In the front row, right in front of Langton, Warren Lash lurched to stand.

No, he wasn't standing.

He'd straightened out in his seat.

One hand flung out, hurling a half-eaten Danish.

His empty coffee cup toppled to the floor.

Langton stopped and stared at Lash, clearly confused.

A fresh kind of fear bubbled up Dale's spine.

Lash's face bloomed a ripe tomato red.

He released a harsh, gurgling cry and collapsed across his fancy little laptop.

One arm twitched.

Then he lay still.

$ git commit murder

Michael Warren Lucas

Tilted
Windmill
Press

I am compelled to thank the hordes of BSD developers who have made me feel welcome over the last two-plus decades. This, right here, is the thanks they get. Maybe it'll teach them a lesson.

I also need to thank Bob Beck, Rob Cornell, Bonnie Koenig, Matthew Kroll, Kate MacLeod, George Neville-Neil, Sharon Reamer, Lucy Snyder, Christina York, and Melissa Yuan-Innes for helping me make this book the best it could be.

This is for Liz.

$ git commit murder

Michael Warren Lucas

Author's Note:

This book takes place in a universe parallel to ours.

I know people like the people in this book. But those people aren't these people. Any characters that share names with real people are used fictionally. The Berkeley Software Distribution community evolved in different a way than what's portrayed in this book. The Byward University of Science and Technology in Ottawa does not exist. There is no BSD North conference, nor, sadly, a BSD Belfast. The security exploits I describe are impossible—uh, that is, highly improbable. I made up the most technically implausible exploits I could imagine. This is not a challenge, so don't feel compelled to go create them.

Git, unfortunately, is very real.

1

Dale thought the lobby of Byward University's main residence hall looked like it was designed to house over-adrenalized post-pubescent howler monkeys.

Who had just discovered that extra-strong Canadian booze.

Which, in all fairness, pretty much was the design specification.

The mottled pale amber tile, with just enough rippling texture to keep water and mud from making the floor totally impassible six months of the year, was clearly chosen for industrial durability first and charm second. A broad glass wall exposed a couple of weirdly young-looking students meandering towards the brick lecture hall across the parking lot. The poured concrete walls had faint swirling trowel marks, a dab of character beneath layers of industrial semi-gloss white. Posters beneath plastic-framed Plexiglas advertised an Ottawa summer concert series, the sexual assault hotline, the Student Learning Resource Center—no, *Centre*. Each proclaimed its message in French and English, both carefully sized for precise balance.

Even in June, during the campus' summer semester (semestre?), the rhythmically humming air conditioning couldn't quite suck away undertones of fresh bleach and cleanser, the Sunday afternoon cover-up of a college dorm's Saturday night. Supposedly the BSD North tech conference was held this time of year specifically because the dormitories and lecture halls were mostly abandoned, but maybe the summer students self-selected for "most likely to not get away with this kind of crap at home."

At least the lobby had a dozen exits, leading out to the pedestrian walkway and the parking lot.

Once, a thirty-foot arch had welcomed everyone straight into the residence hall. In some prior decade, a wooden frame had been fitted into the arch, supporting a sturdy glass wall pierced by two turnstile-guarded doorways. You couldn't walk into the residences without passing straight by fifteen feet of Reception.

Dale Whitehead had seen less solid reception counters at low-rent hotels back home in Detroit. The counter base was some heavy white glossy material, scuffed by years of idly kicking feet, topped with a sea-blue slab that looked like Formica but had to be far tougher.

The tall skinny black guy with the impressive crop of acne working the counter seemed perfectly cheerful as he discussed housing options with a bony kid wearing black—*not really a kid*, Dale reminded himself. He had to be at least twenty, maybe twenty-two. "Ten years younger than Dale" didn't mean a kid, not anymore.

But if you showed up at a university dorm expecting to get a private room, a private bath, and a big-screen TV... you sure weren't a grown-up.

And yet, the guy working the counter seemed perfectly cheerful as he patiently explained that the building didn't have anything like what the kid wanted. Dale guessed it was true, how they said Canadians were too polite. And Canada's capital was probably the most stereotypically Canadian city of all.

Dale released the handle of his brand-new rolling carryon and flexed his stiff fingers. Detroit was one of the few cities in the States that offered direct flights to Ottawa, but he'd had to jam his two hundred and ninety pounds into a cramped seat for two hours, his kneecaps bruisingly crushed against the seat in front of him. The tiny commuter jet was three seats wide, one on the left and two on the right, so he hadn't needed to sit next to anyone, which helped, but every twitch of the stratosphere had knocked the jet like a toy in the bath. Even his favorite Agatha Christie novel hadn't been able to yank his attention away from the constant heaving of the plane and his stomach. Ninety-one minutes on a blind roller coaster hadn't eased Dale's instinctive aversion to flying. His stomach still ached, and clammy sweat still soaked the back of his T-shirt beneath the hefty backpack holding his laptop and other gear.

The crowded, weaving number 97 bus from the airport to Byward hadn't given him an opportunity to still himself.

The lesson there: when you already have motion sickness, don't stand in the back of a tandem cantilevered bus.

At least he'd taken his meds before getting on the plane. A flare of attention deficit disorder would wreck his plans before the con even started.

"You've got to talk to Pete," the man standing behind Dale said. "Get this whole buffer cache thing sorted once and for all."

"Pete does not *want* to talk," the woman said, her thin voice lumbering with a thick Eastern European accent.

"It's the only way you'll work this out," the man said. "Sit at a table with him tonight, with a bunch of us. Have a beer. Talk about something else, anything else. Break the ice."

"Oh, I'll have a beer," the woman said. "Probably on the other side of the bar. His whole page locking model's screwed. I'll need a beer just to get my head around it."

They had to be here for the operating system conference.

Dale should turn around. Say hello. Meet his first conference attendees.

You're here to talk to people. Make contacts. Learn. The convention committee flew you out here to present. That's why the boss told you to come here.

5

But after the tumultuous flight on a jet that should have been labeled "the leaky rowboat of the skies," the interminable wait at Customs, and the nausea-inducing tandem bus, Dale just wanted to get to a room so he could peel out of his sweat-soaked T-shirt and sit in quiet stillness for ten minutes. Give his heart a chance to slow. The roar of the airplane and the bus had faded from his ears, but still echoed inside his skull.

The longer you wait to introduce yourself, the harder it'll be.

Dale made himself swallow. Even his teeth felt greasy. Airport bagels, miraculous things. Bread from anywhere else in the world wouldn't leave your mouth feeling quite that repulsive.

My breath probably smells like puke. My clothes have to stink, after that flight. Not a good first impression.

"We do still have one double room left," the counter guy said. "Two bedrooms with a shared bath. You could rent both sides."

The kid at the counter said, "This is a joke, right? No, never mind— I'll call the hotel down the street. The Royal York, isn't it?"

"As you like, sir. There's a phone book near the pay phone."

Dale couldn't suppress a tiny smile. When Sharon LePlace, the BSD North conference travel coordinator, had informed Dale that speaker accommodations included a shared-bathroom double suite, he'd flinched at the thought of sharing a bath and investigated hotel rooms. With the Canadian Parliament out of session the Royal York had rooms available, and thanks to low demand they'd lowered their rates to a paltry four hundred dollars a night.

But no question the entitled kid would get his private room that way.

The clerk looked up at Dale, relief shading his voice. "Bonjour? Hello?"

Dale tugged his rolling bag forward in relief. "Yes, please." No, that sounded too rough. Just because his flight up here had left him feeling violated didn't mean he should get snappy with this poor college student, who probably worked here to pay his way through this same school. He coughed to reset his voice. "You should have a reservation? Name of Dale Whitehead?" *Dale, you are thirty-two years old. Stop making everything sound like a question, they damn well* better *have a reservation for you.*

The kid clacked at his keyboard. "Are you with a group?"

"BSD North," Dale said. No, that's too harsh again. Sound confident, not like some jerkface American. He tried to relax his shoulders with the weight of his backpack. The motion made the spots on his thick-lensed wire-rim glasses more obvious.

He needed to clean those, too. Maybe a shower, straight away?

"Here you are," the clerk said. "Half a double suite. Room 1408, on the fourteenth floor. Has Mister…" He glanced down. "—Lash come with you?"

"No," Dale said. LaPlace's email had said that his suitemate was Warren Lash, a programmer with the SkyBSD project. Dale had heard the name before, knew he was a project bigwig, but had never interacted with the man. "He's flying in from… Colorado? Some place like that."

"I'm Warren Lash," said the behind Dale. The guy who'd advocated beer.

Don't grimace. You're supposed to be friendly—no, you are friendly, you just have a hard time with people. Dale couldn't quite get a smile on his face as he turned.

Warren Lash was a tall guy with long straight red hair, with a face just picking up middle age fleshiness. He carried his laptop backpack with both straps over one shoulder, a tiny thing, probably holding an Apple or some other triumph of style over power, and a big rolling suitcase festooned with stickers advertising open-source software conferences in places like Serbia and Belize. Despite the darkened semicircles beneath his eyes, he grinned.

Cocky? Friendly? Hard to tell.

"You must be Dale Whitehead," Lash said, holding out a hand. "Utah."

You know how to do this. Pull up the corners of your mouth. Show some teeth, not too much. "It's nice to meet you." Shake the hand, not too limp.

Lash said, clearly travel-worn but full of easy confidence. "This is Marina Unpronounceable."

The woman said something beginning with *str* and a herd of *ch* and *k* and not nearly enough vowels in it.

Dale blinked in bafflement.

Marina sighed. "Em-Day-Ess. SkyBSD."

Dale blinked again, this time in surprise. *mds@skybsd.org.* "You do the crypto storage layers." That was hard stuff.

"Some of them, yes," Marina said.

"Gentlemen," the clerk said. "Let's get you both checked in. Identification?"

By the time Dale fumbled for his wallet and extricated his driver's license from a flurry of receipts—can't lose the receipts, he could expense all of this—Lash had moved up and slipped his license onto the cool laminate counter.

As the receptionist typed Lash looked at Dale and said, "You're doing the talk on wireless IP service using abandoned building rooftops, aren't you?"

He knows who I am. Dale's back tightened as he suddenly felt hunted. "That's right."

"I bet that's going to be a great talk."

Dale swallowed. "I hope so. It's my first time."

"You've never been here before?" Lash said. "Well, welcome."

"Welcome," Marina said.

Of *course* he's welcoming me, Dale thought.

He thinks I'm one of the good guys.

2

Dale's brain ran like a jet engine: wonderful if you wanted to cross the country, but useless for day-to-day life.

Attention deficit disorder didn't disable him. He could concentrate for hours, or even days, so long as nobody interrupted him. He could understand complicated computer code, reading it all into his own brain and silently following forking data paths further than most anyone.

People, though, left him flummoxed and confused.

And it's not like he could explain what was happening in his head. He'd tried, more than once, but by the time he reached high school he'd learned better. People didn't understand. They told him he was wrong, and if he insisted, they pushed him away. Even if they said they wouldn't, they did.

Sometimes he wondered if they rejected him from inability or unwillingness, but it didn't really matter.

So long as he focused his energy on the people around him, he could fake normality. At least until he'd heard too many words, and couldn't make sense of them anymore.

That's why he always watched for the exits. Excusing himself always worked.

Computers were easier. An Internet Relay Chat session had more leeway. If he really screwed up there, he could go to another channel or change his handle.

Dale wished he could change his channel right now, but that wasn't an option for meatspace. He headed for the elevator, Lash at his back.

We're suitemates, going to the same place. It's not like he's stalking me or something. But Dale still had that familiar, uncomfortable itch between his shoulder blades. People talked all the time. What should he be saying? No, Lash was trailing behind, not beside him. He didn't have to say anything.

So long as he acted as if he was on a mission, at least.

It worked until the battered elevator doors slid shut and Lash asked, "How was your trip?"

Dale's stomach twitched again. Who talked in an elevator? "Okay, I guess." He swallowed. "Bit rough." Was the elevator wobbling?

"Oh? I came through Toronto, I must have missed that."

The elevator wobbled to a halt, the doors dinging open. No convenient placard declared which way to which rooms, but a door on the opposite wall had a little flag-like sign sticking out above it, declaring itself number 1401. Room 1402 was just behind it.

"This way," Dale said with relief as Lash's suitcase rattled across the elevator gap.

1403, 1404, all on the left wall. The corridor turned. 1405, 1406, and turned again.

The floor was smaller than Dale had thought.

The corridor was a ring.

Three-quarters of the way around the floor, Dale stopped in front of 1408, hoping his face wasn't burning as much as he thought. "Other way would have been quicker," he made himself say.

"No worries," Lash said. "We all do that," *noise* "year."

Dale's gut clenched harder.

He was already dropping words.

It's just stress, Dale thought. *The guy was being reassuring. You don't have to answer. Go sit down, it'll pass.*

Hoping Lash hadn't noticed the delay, Dale fumbled his swipe card through the reader below the door handle. An LED flashed green.

The right model of swipe card. I own *this building.*

Dale shoved the idea away more firmly than he shoved the door handle, and stepped into a disaster.

3

When the BSD North travel coordinator had said a two-bedroom suite with a shared bath, Dale had imagined a room like he had at college: two bedrooms, side by side, with a bath between them. A door on each end of the bathroom. A solid door. A door that could be locked from the bathroom side, and let Dale pretend that he had his own space.

Byward University's suites were more like two-bedroom apartments, cheerlessly decorated in different shades of white. The front door opened into a kitchen area, complete with glossy white fridge and microwave. The sink's chrome bowl and spigot made a spot of color against the glossy white counter. A sturdy table filled the corner.

An open door exposed the bathroom.

Two more open doors led to bedrooms.

Dale swallowed. A midnight bathroom run meant sneaking through the common room. Yes, everybody used the bathroom—but he couldn't even pretend normality while half-asleep. And was he supposed to have brought a bathrobe for his shower?

Worst of all: every room had only one exit.

If he screwed up talking with Lash he'd have to, what? Go into his bedroom and shut the door?

"Not bad for a university, huh?" Lash said behind him. "Which one would you like? Neither one faces east, that six AM sunrise is a killer."

"I—don't think I care," He'd have to wear his dirty clothes into the bath to take a shower, carry his pajama bottoms with him. He'd need a shirt to go with the pajama pants, though—nobody needed to see his flabby gut.

"You sure?" Lash sounded impatient. "Well, pick one and let's get to the bar."

You're in the way, idiot! Dale took two steps in, towards the room on the right.

Lash trundled past him, dragging that ridiculous suitcase towards the left-hand bedroom.

The door glided shut, hitting with a surprisingly loud thud. A roommate coming home would never surprise you, not with a door like that.

It's not that bad. The con is only two days, Monday and Tuesday. I fly home Wednesday morning. But he should have brought more shirts. He'd soaked through his on the flight, and talking to Lash had made it worse.

Lash dropped the suitcase right inside the bedroom door. "Bar?"

"Uh, bar?"

"Right, first time," Lash said. "Early registration's over at the Royal Oak, tonight. They'll have your badge and T-shirt and stuff. Plus, a lot of folks have been here for a couple days already, what with the SkyBSD and CoreBSD devsummits and the tutorials and all *that* stuff."

Dale's chest tightened. *So I get to try to work myself into a bunch of people who know each other already.* "I've got a couple things to take care of. Told the boss I'd check my email first thing."

"I did that on the bus," Lash said cheerfully. "Canadian SIM card, six gigs for ten bucks, best investment you can make. Come on over when you can, it's out the front door and left down the walkway, it veers a little to the right but straightens out again. Straight down that to the streetlight, it's a crosswalk really, and turn right. Almost two blocks, on the left. Can't miss it. Cross at the crosswalk, it's just easiest. If you don't need a guide, I can call my wife and the kids on the way."

"Thanks," Dale said. Lash seemed perfectly cordial, but spoke so quickly that Dale felt clubbed with friendliness. Really, though, it wouldn't have helped if Lash had spoken in a drawling monotone. "I'll do that."

"See you there," Lash said, slipping past Dale and out the door.

Another thud as the door shut, then blessed silence pressed down on Dale's ears with a rush of tinnitus.

He released the rolling bag's handle and sagged on his feet.

Distant air conditioning heaved, dropping a puff of cooler air over Dale's face. The suite didn't quite smell stale, but nobody had been in here for several days, at least. Not really a pleasant smell, faded bathroom cleaner and dust, but it promised quiet.

Dale shrugged his heavy laptop bag off his shoulders, splashing a sudden shock of coolness across his steaming sweat-soaked back. The backpack didn't quite thud on the ground—too many different parts inside for it to thud—but it landed with a reassuring solidity.

Quiet.

Dale been further from home, once. He'd been eight, in the back seat of the family van. His dad still had pictures of the whole family in front of Mount Rushmore and at the edge of the Grand Canyon. The one of his kid sister Missy, still tiny at six years old, on a dock with her feet dangling in the Mississippi, Dale had hung in his apartment.

His reasons for coming here suddenly felt flimsy. Dale had mentioned the conference to his boss, Will Qwilleran, who had badgered him into submitting a talk proposal. Dale could give technical talks—he'd done any number of them in front of customers before, and even talked at a few user groups around Metro Detroit. A few of those groups recorded all their talks and uploaded them to the Internet, for public consumption.

Will wants me to get the company's name out. The company uses SkyBSD, I've got CoreBSD on my laptop, I know a whole bunch of these guys from online, I was the right person for him to send.

And Dale had his own reasons for going to the conference.

Reasons he didn't dare tell anyone.

But there wasn't *any* way Dale was going to the bar tonight. He'd need all his mental energy to survive the next two days.

He sighed and dragged his suitcase into the bedroom.

The bedroom itself wasn't bad. A thick mattress on a double steel frame, with two heavy pillows and sheets obviously chosen for sturdiness rather than thread count. A heavy pole lamp by the bed, a battered laminate desk built in underneath the tinted window spanning the west wall, the chair situated so you got an incredible view of Byward University's rooftop air conditioners. An alcove held a wire-frame shelf with a closet bar beneath it.

The bedroom door didn't have a lock.

At least it closed solidly.

Dale put his rolling bag on its side, beside the desk, and flung it open, exposing tightly-crammed clothes and toiletries. With acute disgust he yanked his sweat-filled T-shirt over his head, wadded it up, and dropped it in the empty suitcase top. The cool rush over his flabby chest and gut felt wonderful.

There. Dale had brought five T-shirts: two for Monday, two for Tuesday, and one for Wednesday's flight home. Without a clean shirt, he wasn't going anywhere tonight.

Dale dragged his feet out of his overheated black sneakers, delighting in the cool rush between his toes, imagining the fetid steam that must be rising from the shoes' depths.

Maybe the thing to do was take his shower now. He really didn't feel hungry, not after that horrible flight. Just skip dinner. He had a couple of protein bars in his laptop backpack. That way he'd be out of the bathroom before Lash returned.

Geeks in a bar? Heck, he might be *asleep* before Lash returned.

Avoid the whole problem for another day.

That was a plan he could live with.

This whole trip had been a terrible idea.

Before he did anything, though, he needed to cool down. Clear his brain. Find a way to relax. Find something that made him feel… safer.

Dale didn't let himself think about what that would be.

Instead, he hoisted the laptop bag onto the desk to make it happen.

4

Dale had built his laptop himself, using parts he'd ordered straight from Asian factories: two processors on a thoughtfully hand-selected motherboard, seventeen-inch ultra-high-res screen, enough hard drive to hold the good bits of the Library of Congress and enough memory to keep all the files in use off the disk. A full-size keyboard, including a number pad. The burnished aluminum case was the expensive part— Dale's high school buddy Brian made them, in the fabricating shop in his family's barn.

He pressed the power button. White text flashed past on the black screen while he rooted through the tangle of cables for the power cord. He really had to organize this mess. The Velcro cable ties were sitting on the shelf at home, he just had to sit down and coil everything up nicely. But before the laptop hit the logon screen, he had the laptop plugged in.

Most computers booted to a pretty logon screen with, say, a soothing shade of blue and a welcoming invitation to type your password. Maybe a picture of a flower or a kitten in the background. Something that promised a pleasant, even fun experience.

This laptop's logon screen was black, displaying the word "Login" and a colon in the upper left corner.

People told Dale his computer didn't look friendly. Dale always said it was perfectly friendly—it just was choosy about who its friends were. The BSD Unix operating systems dated from the early days of computing, when a "portable computer" came with wheels and a hernia belt. Descendants of that software ran the core of the Internet, and didn't cost a penny. Yes, some people used commercial variants from big companies like IBM, and other people liked other free operating systems, but Dale liked the stability, performance, and sense of history this system gave him.

Dale entered his username—*dsw*, for Dale Shirley Whitehead— and the meaningless mishmash of two dozen characters and letters and symbols that served as his password. The computer rewarded him with another blank screen and a single symbol.

$

The laptop had finished saying its piece. Now it was Dale's chance to begin a dialog.

The room around Dale faded as he connected to the *Byward Guest* wireless network and connected to his home system. His powerful laptop was now only a screen and keyboard, funneling what Dale typed to a small computer in his bedroom closet. He had that computer connect him to still another machine.

Dale had found this system last month. As far as he could tell, it was in Indonesia, or maybe Malaysia, and handled a dozen email accounts for a small company. The company's computer staff hadn't applied security patches since setting the system up last year. Dale hadn't found breaking into it difficult at all.

Dale wasn't exactly a hacker. Lots of people would have used this unknown company's email server to, say, knock competitors off of online gaming sites, or maybe express their annoyance with whatever mega-corporation had displeased them. Dale had broken in, yes, but he'd cleaned the server up. If the server was a house, Dale was an uninvited guest who nonetheless fixed the broken windows and put the rear door back on its hinges. Yes, he'd set the system to not log his activity, but that was basic self-protection.

And he made absolutely sure the system owners got their e-mail.

Otherwise, they might call someone to fix the machine.

Really, he provided them a service.

He had maybe a dozen machines like this, all over the world.

And if everything went well this week, Dale would have a few million more machines at his disposal.

A million places to hide, to get away, where nobody would think to look for him.

Dale loved computers. He loved the layers of understanding you needed to really get them, all the way up from the NAND gate to the Java Runtime Engine. A billion billion details, yes—but ultimately knowable. If you were smart enough, if you studied enough, you could understand all the rules. You could predict exactly what the machine would do.

Exactly unlike people.

Penetrating these systems only meant that he understood them better than the person supposedly responsible for them.

He might be trapped in Ottawa.

But on a mental level, nobody could find him.

He'd escaped without leaving his assigned room.

Dale had that system forward his connection to a similar system in the Czech Republic, then one somewhere in Canada. He'd secured each of those neglected machines and erased his footprints, but on this last computer he'd installed a bunch of tools he could use for his own purposes.

Like getting back into the Byward University network.

Focusing on the task at hand rather than what it meant, Dale slipped commands through a gap into the Byward University facilities network—not the student network, but the network used to support the university infrastructure, like the lights and heat.

And the residence hall registration system.

With a connection dragged around the world, through who knew how many different networks, the latency between typing a letter and that letter appearing on the screen drove Dale to keep his mind blank to starve his impatience. He waited for the full text of each command to appear before hitting ENTER, so that a misplaced keystroke wouldn't damage the fragile chain of connections.

Even with the lag, Dale quickly found the entry for his registration: his full name, the conference schedule, dates, and most important—the twenty-four-digit numerical identifier for his key card.

He copied that number.

Another burst of typing brought up the list of administrative key cards issued to janitors, housekeepers, and maintenance men. These cards opened every lock in the building.

Dale couldn't just add his card to the list. A sharp-eyed administrator would certainly notice a list of seventy-four items suddenly becoming seventy-five.

But he could identify a card that hadn't been used in three months.

And substitute his number in its place.

The key card in Dale's pants pocket suddenly felt warm.

It's not that Dale *wanted* to open any card-controlled door in the residence hall.

But if things went bad, if he screwed up talking to people and *had* to flee, he could.

The tension bled out of Dale's back. A breath he hadn't realized he'd been holding sagged out of his chest, and he worked his jaw to unclamp it.

Backing down the chain of computers was easier than getting in. Holding down the control key and repeatedly hitting D logged him out of Byward University, then out of the Canadian relay, the Czech one, and Indonesia, each computer responding more quickly than the one before it.

Dale might be among strangers a thousand miles from home, but he was logged onto his home computer.

If you can't escape in meatspace, get away in cyberspace.

The worn plastic chair chilled his clammy back, and the vaguely stale air burned in his nose. Dale rolled his shoulders, trying to break up the knots in his back, and sipped flat airport water from the half-empty bottle stuffed in the side of his backpack.

Now his email. He'd tried a bunch of the fancy mail clients, but kept going back to the text-only simplicity of mutt.

He answered Mom first, reassuring her that he'd made it to Ottawa just fine and the flight had been just fine and that he was, really and truly, just fine. A couple cousins sending pictures, those could wait. A couple social network messages—you've been tagged, we love you, return to us! Delete, delete, delete. Those social media companies still couldn't improve on the Internet Relay Chat computer geeks had used for decades.

Dale's boss Will had sent an email half an hour ago, though. He'd probably better actually read that.

Dale,

I've been to many tech conferences. There is a bar. There is _always_ a bar.

You're there to make contacts. We need these people kindly disposed towards us. Get out of your room. I expect expense reports, remember? And they better have other people's drinks on them. Get those problem reports closed.

:WQ

Well, crap.

Dale was gonna need more shirts.

5

Fresh deodorant, mouthwash, and Monday morning's T-shirt didn't make Dale feel much better. He tested his keycard as he slipped out of the room—yep, it still worked, even with his changes. Robbed of that excuse to delay, he rode the elevator down and slunk out. The late afternoon sun stabbed out of the western sky into his aching eyes as he trudged down the walkway towards the bar Lash had mentioned.

Unfortunately, the directions were too simple for him to forget.

The Royal Oak bar looked like it had been a Victorian manor, two looming stories of oversized red bricks encumbered with miles of hungry ivy. They'd poured a concrete deck around the whole thing, right up to the sidewalk, and put a wooden rail fence around the border. The deck was about half full of people clustered around tables, talking loudly and gesturing over tall curvy glasses of beer and platters of fried heaven. Dale saw a couple people wearing T-shirts bearing the

BSD North logo over the breast loitering on the sidewalk just outside the patio, chattering at each other as they sucked cigarettes.

This had to be the place.

The afternoon wasn't that warm—Ottawa in June seemed less torrid than Detroit, the air a few degrees cooler and dry—but even without dragging his rolling bag and hoisting his backpack, Dale already felt that telltale dampness under his armpits. His breath struggled against the lump blocking his throat.

Lash had mentioned registration. Probably the place to start. And a conference T-shirt would solve his clothing shortage, assuming they had one big enough for him.

One of the smokers nodded and smiled as Dale tromped past them towards the recessed entrance.

Dale tried to smile back, but was pretty sure it looked bogus.

At least Ontario had banned smoking indoors. His asthma wouldn't detonate.

The bar might have been a Victorian manor once, but the inner walls were almost all knocked out except behind the high wooden bar, leaving dark hardwood floors and plaster walls painted a pale cream, the closest you could get to white and still conceal burger-greasy handprints. The ceiling looked a little darker—probably an underlying patina of decades of cigarette smoke. A large screen TV over the bar displayed two teams in unfamiliar uniforms knocking a soccer ball back and forth. While the broadcast was thankfully muted, the knots of people around tiny haphazard wooden tables raised a rumble that assaulted Dale's ears. Many wore tech conference T-shirts: BSD North, TokyoBSD, USENIX, SANS, Linux World, and more. One scrawny man on the edge of elderly, with thinning blond hair and an absurdly long, drooping mustache curled at the ends, wore a faded white T-shirt that read FREE THE BERKELEY 4.4, the red daemon mascot worn almost to invisibility—that had to be twenty years old. Even those that didn't wear T-shirts, like the tall lanky man in a ridiculous sport jacket, white shirt, and tightly knotted red tie, seemed informal. The man in the sports jacket leaned close to hear his tablemates expostulate. Dale's ears, already abused by the flight, barely picked out a few scraps of conversation.

"—get some poutine while we're—"

"—a *real* database for packages, not some flat file with an SQL interface—"

"—the Keat's, that's a *proper* ale—"

"—commit bit, he's earned—"

He couldn't follow a single discussion thread if he wanted to.

Not that anybody would really be interested in talking to him.

Worse, the enticing smells of fried hamburgers and fried potatoes and fried—fried *everything* hooked into Dale's nose, making his stomach grumble.

Twenty minutes ago you were full of knots, Dale told his stomach. *Knock it off, you don't get fried this trip. You get stupid healthy stuff like, like… bugs. Bugs and gravel.*

His stomach grumbled again.

Dale glanced around, quite overwhelmed. He avoided bars on busy nights, preferring quieter evenings where he could have an actual conversation with co-workers or old friends. The urge to turn and walk away flared brightly. *If I can't find registration, I'll go back to my room.*

Over to the left, opposite the bar, a few small square tables sat right up against each other, stacked high with flat red cloths. A slightly pudgy bald guy sat behind them, fingers dancing through a box of index cards as a tired-looking man in jeans and a faded blue-stripe dress shirt looked on.

That's it. Dammit.

The man introduced himself as Ian Langton, conference chair. Dale accepted a lanyard badge, a cheap cloth bag of sponsor ads, and a size 3X T-shirt.

"First time here, I believe?" Langton said.

"That's right." Dale silently chanted *Ian Langton, Ian Langton* as he studied the man's face, trying to cram the name so tightly into his brain that it wouldn't fall out.

"Glad you made it. We always want new speakers." Langton flipped a couple pages on a clipboard and made a check next to an entry, marking off Dale's name. "It's the biggest BSD North ever, almost five hundred people registered."

The *last* thing Dale needed to know. "Thanks."

"You'll be on right after the keynote," Langton said.

At least it'll be over quick.

His ID badge gave his name in capitals, DALE WHITEHEAD, and his company name beneath that in italics: *Detroit Network Services.*

Dale stepped aside to let a guy built like Jupiter—the planet, not the god—sign in. He got the badge into the holder with a minimum of struggle and hung the whole thing around his neck. It dangled right at the top of his gut, at just enough of an angle to highlight his paunch. Perfect.

He was in. Now for the hard problem.

The bewildering crowd shifted around tables like seaweed rolling with the tide. Faces huddled around tables, speaking loudly to be heard over a hundred other loud conversations, close enough to smell each other's breath. After that flight, mouthwash or no, Dale probably smelled like malignant bagel and heaved bile.

He could go back to his room. Order carryout Chinese and a bunch of booze. Expense the whole thing.

No, Will would know. Will always figured things out. He'd ask a couple questions, and Dale would blow the whole story.

Computers were easy.

How do you hack into a room full of people you don't know?

At a table near the patio doors, yet another skinny bald guy in black raised a hand at Dale.

Dale furrowed his eyebrows, puzzled.

The bald guy's tablemate, a slightly older and more heavy-set guy with a short black beard, pivoted to look at Dale and said something to his tablemate.

Who were these people?

The bald guy waved for him to come over.

Dale's face must have shown his confusion. The bald guy nodded and waved. The bearded guy nodded in confirmation.

Dale took a deep breath, clenched the con bag's flimsy handles like a drowning man seizing a rope, and wove through the crowd to the beckoning strangers.

6

"You look like you're new here," the bearded guy said, raising his voice above the discussions in the tightly-packed tables around them. He wore a polo shirt with a sharply creased collar, thin-lensed wire-rimmed glasses hanging from the bottom button.

Dale nodded. "First time." He felt painfully aware of the tiny table a fraction of an inch directly behind him, the four youngsters sitting around it eating massive burgers and arguing compilers, cumbersome GCC versus the comparatively sleek Clang.

Dale's innards grumbled uneasily. He clamped down. He was *not* going to start a tech conference by farting all over someone's dinner.

"Great!" The bearded guy spoke English with a vaguely British accent. "Have a seat. I'm Brian, Brian Mallard. Maybe you can help us."

The skeleton-skinny hairless man in an expensive black skin-tight sleeveless shirt held out a hand. "Gerry Peterson."

Here we go. But at least the name was familiar. Dale had seen Peterson's name on the SkyBSD mailing lists, usually trying to make some point about usability. Dale pulled out the empty seat and plopped down. "Dale Whitehead."

"Welcome to BSD North," Mallard said. "Are you with a project?"

"Just a happy customer," Dale said, trying to study Mallard's face without being too obvious about it. *Brian Mallard. Brian Mallard.* "Sent a few patches, a few problem reports, here and there." He folded his forearms across the warm, almost sticky varnished tabletop.

"Perfect," Peterson said.

A brand new trepidation whispered in the back of Dale's brain. "For what?"

"We're having an… an argument," Mallard said, leaning a little closer and dropping his voice a couple decibels.

"Discussion," Peterson said.

"Opinionated discussion," Mallard said.

"And we need a random neutral contributor off the street," Peterson said.

Dale studied Peterson's face. Peterson, Peterson—what was his first name, damn it? How did *anyone* remember all these names? "Okay," Dale said. "I can be random."

That didn't sound nearly as clever outside his head as it had inside.

But Peterson's lips twitched in a vanishing smile—not actual amusement, but just enough to acknowledge that Dale had a sense of humor.

Someone tapped Dale's shoulder.

Dale jumped.

The squat waiter said, a little loudly to penetrate the crowd, "Can I get you something?"

"God, yes," Dale said. *Peterson, Mallard. And… Langton, that's it.*

"Yep, he's a BSD guy," Mallard said.

"*What* can I get you?" the waiter said with exaggerated patience.

"Uh…" Dale's brain scrabbled. He knew what the bar at home carried, and what he liked there. But this was Canada, everything was kind of weird over here. Maybe a Labatt? No, that was, like, Generic Canadian Beer, he might as well tattoo a big L on his forehead. What did he want? A beer would take some of the edge off, but the press of people made it almost impossible to think. His brain scrabbled through what he'd seen at the bar, the scraps of conversation he'd overheard—

"Keat's?" Dale said.

"Pale, dark, or red?" the waiter said.

On those occasions that Dale went to the bar, he usually had a Bud from tap. But he wasn't going to admit ignorance right off. "Pale." That sounded decisive, like he knew what he was doing. Worst case, he got a crap beer.

"Right away," the waiter said.

Mallard leaned in. "So. Speaking as an occasional SkyBSD contributor, how do you find the bug report process?"

What was Mallard getting at? When the operating system misbehaved, you took notes and debugging output and sent it in. "Uh, it's fine, I guess."

"It could be better?" Peterson said.

"Anything can be better," Dale said. He itched for his beer, just to have something to do with his hands.

"Would you contribute more if it was easier?" Peterson said.

"All the easy bugs are fixed," Dale said.

Mallard snorted.

"But as a contributor," Peterson said. "As a person who's not part of the cabal—"

"There is no SkyBSD cabal," Mallard said.

Peterson waved a hand. "Whatever. What's your experience of filing bug reports?"

Dale swallowed. He felt attention was like one of those big concave solar stoves; sitting at the focal point made him feel increasingly warm. Getting grilled wasn't comfortable, but at least it had got him a place at a table. He could tell Qwilleran than he'd talked to people at the bar right after he arrived, and what they'd talked about. "Uh, I notice when something goes wrong. If it's a kernel panic, I get a dump. If it's a program crash, or just a Principle of Least Astonishment failure, I run it in verbose mode, with all the debugging turned on. See if I can reproduce it. I look at the source code, to see why the system behaves that way." Dale tried to concentrate through the surrounding clamor. "If I can fix it myself, I upload the patch to Bugzilla and wait to see if anyone bothers to take it."

Peterson slapped the table, the noise dull in the hubbub. "Right there. That's it, right there."

"Git is not going to solve the patch problem," Mallard said.

Dale relaxed. He'd been called into a version control software argument.

Version control software was almost as old as software itself, allowing developers to keep track of source code changes. Different version control programs had their devotees, each insisting that their choice was better than all others.

The original Berkeley BSD code had used SCCS and RCS for version control. SkyBSD and CoreBSD started with CVS, the 1990s standard, on servers accessible to the whole Internet. Eventually SkyBSD had switched to Subversion.

And for the last year or so, an increasing complement of SkyBSD contributors had called for their project to switch to the popular new favorite, Git.

Version control systems didn't just change how the code displayed on a web page. They controlled how people worked. Suggesting a version control system change was like suggesting that the tax people identify people by fingerprint instead of Social Security number, and that returns be delivered by camel rather than the post office. Discussions on the email lists ran for dozens or hundreds of increasingly heated messages, ranging from "this would cause all sorts of problems" to "try it and see why all the cool people like it" to "the CoreBSD buggers still use CVS so you should be happy you even get Subversion" to "this is the twenty-first century." Eventually someone broke out "just because the dumb kids do it," one of those kids shot back with "geezers who think a 386 math coprocessor is still the bomb," and someone from the SkyBSD Senate had to step in and squash the discussion before it turned bloody.

And a whole bunch of those arguments had ended with "let's hash this out at BSD North."

Despite the ease of worldwide communication, despite email and forums and chat and FaceSpace and everything else, nothing beat a face-to-face discussion.

"Look." Peterson waved his half-full glass stein in one hand. "People submit patches, and they sit in Bugzilla for days. Getting them in the repo means that someone has to download the patch, apply it to their tree and test it. Git takes a bunch of that away."

"About half a minute of it," Mallard said. "We still need to test, to build, to figure out if the patch is good."

"Have you even used git?" Peterson said.

Mallard rolled his eyes, looking increasingly impatient. "Everyone's used it. It's a tangled nightmare. All those insane commands—I mean, what is the difference between a git commit and a git push? Does anyone really know?"

"Sure," Peterson said. "Use commit when it's—"

Mallard waved a hand. "That's not the point. Git raises the bar for contributing. Look at Dale here."

Dale had just started to relax, but jerked to alertness. "What about me?"

"What do you think of git?" Mallard said.

Dale glanced between the two intent faces. "First, all VCS are awful."

Peterson chuckled. "The only thing worse than version control is not having version control."

"Yep," Mallard said.

"But," Dale said, "there's not that much git I have to know."

"Are you a committer anywhere?" Mallard asked.

Dale raised a hand. "Oh, no." A committer could change the public source code of one of these projects. "I just send patches."

"Not for lack of trying," said a voice behind Dale.

7

Dale jumped in surprise, bumping the flimsy bar table.

Mallard and Peterson grabbed their beer glasses.

"Dale Whitehead you must be," rumbled the burly man at Dale's elbow. He wore a pristine white T-shirt with the words "ShufflSoft" in big blocky letters, with the words "21st-Century Web" beneath them. The cotton shirt's chest and sleeves strained against his dockworker biceps.

"Uh," Dale said. How could anyone here know who he was? His stomach spasmed like he'd swallowed a hedgehog. At least he hadn't knocked over a beer in surprise. "Hello?"

"Misha Pokotylo," he said. "Your Twitter profile pic, not bad. Not as pasty as you, but not bad."

Dale's hedgehog dissolved. He'd talked to Pokotylo more than once online. "Oh, right." He held up a hand. "Nice to meet you."

"Meet in meat, yes?" Pokotylo chuckled.

"Take a seat," Mallard said.

Peterson held out a hand at the only empty chair, directly across from Dale. "Yeah, cop a squat."

"Spasebaw." Pokotylo barely fit in the space between the table and the incredibly fat guy sitting directly behind him. While everyone had to talk a little loud to hear over all the surrounding discussions, Pokotylo's voice boomed unnecessarily. "Just flew in from Sodom. Is not my arms that are tired."

Inwardly, Dale cringed. He'd exchanged emails with Pokotylo many times, always on the way the ShufflSoft web application framework worked. They'd never had personal contact.

Pokotylo's comment repelled Dale. It felt just like the crap he took when he admitted that he had ADD—except women had a harder time hiding it.

Worse, Mallard and Peterson had just met Dale.

Sleaze by association.

Peterson glanced at Dale.

Dale wanted to slide under the table. He might as well go home now.

Mallard gave a weak chuckle.

Peterson said, "Cool it with that, Misha. There are women here."

Pokotylo raised a doubting eyebrow and glanced around, the question implied.

"We have half a dozen women speakers this year," Peterson said. "Another dozen pre-registered. There's enough sexist bullshit in tech, we don't need any more."

"Fine, fine." Pokotylo flapped his hand. "Is joke. But fine."

"Just don't do it again," Peterson said.

"I make note to look for Dale here," Pokotylo said. "He sends my crew too many patches. I tell them I fix."

That's right, Dale remembered—Pokotylo wasn't just a part of the team that build the ShufflSoft framework. He was one of the leading members.

What's more, the ShufflSoft patches were part of why Dale had come. Why he'd mentioned BSD North to his boss in the first place.

Even if Dale hadn't said his most honest reason for his interest in ShufflSoft.

Dale's pulse kicked up another notch. "Sorry. I can keep them to myself."

"Nyet!" Pokotylo said. "No no no. You do good work. You fix many problems."

"Uh, thanks," Dale said, the hot point of attention burning the back of his neck again.

"That why you need commit bit."

Surprise flooded Dale. For a big project like ShufflSoft, commit access meant that the people in charge of the software would let him change their project. He'd be able to make those changes himself, directly. So long as he didn't break anything, thousands of people would automatically use his changes.

A software project only gave very trusted people commit bits.

But commit access meant people would not only use his work, they'd see his name attached to it.

Commit access meant uncomfortable exposure.

The more people looked at him, they more they might notice that he didn't really fit in anywhere.

Dale wanted ShufflSoft to make his changes. But he didn't want those changes directly tied to him.

"I send you email tonight," Pokotylo said. "Get you set up. You have crypto keys, right? PGP, SSH?"

"Uh," Dale said. His work, out in public, with his name on it. It was like running through the room naked, but the room was everyone in the world who used that software. "I—I don't think I'm a great fit for you guys."

"Why ever not?" Pokotylo said.

Peterson leaned toward the discussion, interested. Mallard sipped his dwindling beer.

"I just…"

The waitress appeared at that moment, slipping a tall glass of foam-capped yellow beer in front of Dale. "Here you go, honey." Her attention switched to Pokotylo. "What can I get for you?"

Pokotylo opened his mouth to say something, eyed Peterson, and closed it again. "Beer," he said in a beat. "Guinness. Much Guinness."

"You got it."

"Another Blue for me," Mallard said, hoisting his almost drained glass.

"Blue and Guinness. Any food?"

"One of those appetizer platters," Peterson said. "For the table. The big one, with the skins and the wings."

Dale's stomach gave a whole different twitch. Cheesy potato skins sounded fantastic, but he'd sworn off all that stuff for this trip. He needed a salad, or maybe grilled chicken.

"Oooh," Mallard said. "Add some nachos." He glanced around the table. "Nachos okay with you guys?"

Will said I had to network. Looks like I'm committed. "Sure," Dale said. His treasonous mouth watered. "Sounds good."

Dale would have to eat even better for the rest of the week. The suite had a fridge. Maybe he could find a grocery store, find some protein shakes that didn't taste too much like wolverine diarrhea.

Pokotylo nodded. "I flew twenty hours to get here. Could eat cow."

"Nachos with meat or without?" the waitress asked.

"We're not barbarians," Mallard said. "With meat, of course."

She flashed a luminous smile. "You got it."

Pokotylo eyed the retreating waitress for a second as she weaved through the narrow gap between the next tables over, letting Dale catch a breath before continuing, "So. Commit bit. For you."

"Look," Dale said. "I don't run big web sites. I'm not even—and no offense here, really—I'm not really interested in how web servers work." *I don't want my work out in the world, not with my name on it.*

"Is okay." Pokotylo waved a hand. "You find bugs nobody else finds."

"That's just because my network is weird," Dale said quickly. "I sure don't have a million hits a second or anything like that."

"Pfft!" Pokotylo said. "We have many people run big sites. FaceSpace, whatever they're called, they use us. But you—you, your weird network, you find stuff nobody else can find. You fix that. Your fixes, they help other people with weird network."

"What kind of network do you run?" Mallard said.

"I'm with Detroit Network Services," Dale said. The rehearsed words came easily, from long practice. "We provide wired and wireless Internet service through most of Michigan."

"Ah," Peterson said. "You're doing *that* talk."

"Tomorrow, they say," Dale said.

"Right after keynote's the best time to talk," Peterson said. "Everyone's fresh and ready, nobody's even hung over."

Dale glanced around at the crowded tables, innumerable nerdy men raising beer glasses, a few geeky women wedged in between them, waitstaff moving between tables balancing trays heavily laden with brimming glasses. The crowd had already spilled more beer than Dale drank in a month.

"This?" Mallard said, catching Dale's look. "This is *nothing*. Wait until the closing night bash."

"So," Pokotylo said. "You not change subject. Business, then beer. You commit your own fixes, right? Stop with the git pull requests."

"See?" Peterson said to Mallard. "Git again."

"How do I know it's right?" Dale said. "I mean, you want me to just put things out there?"

Mallard said, "The git part doesn't matter. They like his patches."

"All you send this year is good." Pokotylo's eyes stayed on Dale's, giving Dale an uneasy tickle up and down the back of his skull. "You have question, you ask on mailing list. Like you do right now."

"But git makes taking his patches easier," Peterson said.

"But..." Dale's reluctance wavered.

Getting commit access was an honor. It meant the people who ran the project had studied his code. They not only approved of the code, they approved of the skills and reasoning of the person who had produced the code.

But commit access brought a loss of plausible deniability.

If someone else approved of Dale's bug fixes and improvements enough to take them, it meant he'd done his work correctly.

It meant people thought his work was harmless.

Dale sagged. "Look, I'll think about it, okay?"

"And they're still dumping it back on him," Mallard said.

"I send you email tonight," Pokotylo said with satisfaction. "You have what, forty? Fifty pull requests we haven't taken? You handle those, okay? I sit with you, first few times. Make certain you don't molest hound."

Molest hound? Oh, screw pooch, right.

Dale realized he was chewing his lower lip and made himself stop. "Fine."

Direct access to make his own changes didn't ruin all of Dale's plans.

Not really.

Yes, Dale's patches fixed real performance problems that people really experienced.

They had a side effect, though. He'd carefully tuned the way his ShufflSoft patches handled memory. His SkyBSD patches also tuned memory handling. If Dale got his changes into both ShufflSoft and SkyBSD, they'd grant him access to any machine running both sets of software.

About one Internet server in ten ran SkyBSD.

Maybe one in ten of those ran ShufflSoft.

It'd take a while for everyone to upgrade all their systems. But once they did, Dale would have access to one percent of all hosts on the Internet.

Nobody would ever find him.

It's not that Dale planned to bring down the Internet. For all its warts, the Internet was his life.

But gaining access to one percent of the Internet? Even if he never used it?

Now *that* would be cool.

As far as Dale knew, nobody had ever figured out this particular class of software security exploit. Nothing remains secret forever, though. Eventually, some bright kid would figure out what Dale had done.

Without an intermediary to take the fall, the world would certainly blame Dale.

As they should.

8

A thud at the table jerked Dale out of his reverie.

A kid had pulled up a chair to the far side of the table and scooted up. The innumerable buttons pinned to his denim jacket glittered beneath the bar's can lights.

"Guys," Mallard said, "Jason Hellman. Jason, you know Gerry. This is Misha, and Dale."

How does he remember names so easily?

Fortunately, names quickly became irrelevant around the tightly packed table. The discussion turned to operating system support for newer networking congestion control features. Dale found discussing the advantages and disadvantages of changing core Internet protocols far more comfortable than discussing himself, and quickly got sucked into arguing the finer points of obscure implementation details.

Mallard saw a friend and split away, letting a skinny geezer from Los Angeles claim his spot. Someone grabbed another chair to squeeze himself into the side, then their table got slid over to join the next four-top table for a good-natured argument about managing add-on software. Dale got introduced to a bewildering array of faces, with an overwhelming variety of accents.

The only point everyone agreed on was that absolutely everything in computing was absolutely terrible.

About nine o'clock, the warm glow of too many potato skins and nachos and hot wings and deep-fried dill pickle slices seeping through him, Dale found himself yawning widely enough to split his skull. The bar had grown even more crowded. Nobody showed any signs of leaving, but his back still ached from the horrific flight to Ottawa.

Dale glimpsed his suitemate Lash crowded around a table at the back of the room, gesticulating wildly with one hand while holding a beer unnaturally steady in the other. He seemed to be arguing intently with a stocky ponytailed guy in a bright red T-shirt.

Lash'd be there a while.

This was Dale's chance.

Dale quietly muttered "excuse me" and started weaving through the crowd towards the exit.

Twice before Dale reached the door, people whose names he'd already forgotten held up a hand to intercept him. "Heading home already?" "Come on, we've just started!" Each time, Dale offered a fake-feeling smile and said "No, thanks, I'm worn out."

The conference crowd had spilled out onto the sidewalk, tight knots of people in their own conversations. The sky was a brilliant deep blue, with pink still hugging the west between blocky office towers. The cool June breeze caught Dale's shirt, abruptly chilling his sweaty skin. The bar had been warm—no, downright *steamy*.

But in another couple of minutes, Dale achieved escape velocity and headed back down dark sidewalks to the Byward University residence hall, thoughtful.

Much to his surprise… he'd had fun.

Dale loved computing for its depth and predictability. He loved how he could make such a complex machine do whatever he wanted, provided he was willing to understand enough. He enjoyed new challenges, learning new things, and discovering ways to make the system work that nobody had before.

And BSD North seemed full of people who shared those joys.

Yes, hearing had been difficult. His ears still rang from the noise, especially after the battering they'd taken during the flight. And his gut felt Thanksgiving-stuffed—he'd eaten way too much, and three beers really was way more than he needed. He'd tried the Guinness at the urging of a British guy, and found it completely different from what got sold under that name back in Detroit—heavier, richer, more flavorful. "It's not a patch on what we get at home, you understand," the Brit had said, "but Americans think it's—what's the word—*awesome*. Come out to BSD Belfast, we'll arrange *proper* Guinness."

Belfast. Like he'd survive a flight that long without a heart attack.

The buzz in Dale's head didn't come from beer, though. He'd learned all sorts of fascinating computing details, from people who worked in the field and who built operating systems. Walking through streaks of shadows and pools of lamplight between granite-clad school buildings, a million new facts rattled around Dale's brain.

He'd had that kind of discussion before, occasionally, at some of the local user groups. Despite the jokes, some pretty smart people lived in Detroit. Some of the user groups attracted visitors from Silicon Valley or New York.

But here, a whole bunch of the smartest brains in the world had gathered in one bar.

Dale's boss might have been right, the bastard.

Dale might actually enjoy the conference.

The thought made him want to curse.

But he still didn't want to share the bathroom.

The tiny residence suite echoed with Dale's footsteps. He scurried quickly to snatch his toiletries and pajama pants and duck into the tiny bathroom. Dale's elbows could hit both sides of the shower stall simultaneously, as if the stall had been designed to discourage college students from sharing. Even with the bathroom door locked and steaming water pounding his abused muscles, Dale couldn't help listening for the sound of the suite's door opening—or, worse, the bathroom.

For all Dale knew, Lash might stagger in completely blasted, right now.

Puke on the floor right in front of the shower.

Then pass out in the mess, face-down.

A quick scrub, a quicker rinse, and Dale was back in his room.

The bedroom door didn't lock, but wedging the desk chair under the handle sapped just a bit of the tension from his shoulders. The only sounds were the distant susurrus of the air conditioning seeping through the age-grimed vent. Dale would have preferred an open window, but the tiny sliding portal in the corner of the window was only big enough to admit the grumble of buses and a tiny breeze thick with diesel fumes, so he left it shut.

The mattress would have violated the "cruel and unusual punishment" clause of the US Constitution, but apparently Canadians didn't have that rule, at least for college students. Dale propped both pillows—each as plush and soft as rolled-up jeans—up against the wall, squirmed until he aligned the knots in his back between the mattress' lumps, and spent an hour reading the new Rob Cornell novel before double-checking his seven AM alarm and turning off the light.

Tomorrow, he gave his presentation.

Five hundred people at the conference. How many of those cared about makeshift wireless in the ghetto of Detroit?

And Dale felt pretty sure there wouldn't be beer to help him break his way in.

And commit access.

Everything he did, exposed.

Plus, sheets that had maybe three threads per inch.

Sore from the flight and sprawled on the annoyingly lumpy mattress, he expected to spend the night tossing and turning.

Instead, minutes later, sleep sucked him down.

9

A noxious, distant klaxon made Dale crack an eye.

The morning light seeping through a gap in the heavy curtain nailed the eyelid open.

Dale's tongue tasted like raw meat left on the kitchen counter overnight. In August. The lumps in the mattress had migrated into his back. Sometime in the night he'd thrown the coarse sheet down, his slow nocturnal kicks and flops twisting the burlap-like cotton into manacles.

He rolled an aching arm over to the desk where he'd plugged in his phone to charge.

Six forty-five AM. Fifteen minutes before his own alarm went off.

On the other side of the suite's thin wall, someone groaned.

Warren Lash? Had to be.

The klaxon silenced.

Star Trek, Dale thought through the sleep oozing through his brain. *Red alert. Original series.*

At least Lash had taste.

Next door, Lash groaned again.

Feet hit the thinly carpeted floor.

Dale suddenly felt utterly exposed. The door to his room was snugly closed, the office chair still tilted under the knob. The heavy plastic-lined window drape was pulled tight. Nobody could see Dale in his flimsy cotton PJ pants, pale flabby gut hanging out. Still, Dale couldn't help reaching down to tug at the sheet, stealthily twisting his ankles until the cloth came free and he could pull it protectively over his chest.

How had he slept through Lash coming in last night? The dorm's front door closed with a thud like a bank vault, and the interior walls had all the soundproofing of a cheap tent. Dale must have been more tired than he'd thought.

The fatigue wasn't just the flight, or the nauseating bus ride. Listening to everyone last night had been work, unaccustomed mental labor. His brain felt tired.

But listening to Lash fumble out of his own room, Dale felt much better about returning to the dorm room early. Lash, obviously, had stayed out far too late. And judging from Lash's irregular footsteps as he lurched towards the suite's bathroom, he'd also had far more than Dale's three beers.

Listening to a stranger shower was exactly as horribly intimate as it had been in college.

But he could lie there until Lash came out and get caught in his PJs, or get up and get dressed and meet Lash wearing pants.

By the time Dale finished running his electric razor over his morning stubble, Lash had abandoned the bathroom and returned to his room. Dale worked his tongue between his cheeks, scowled in revulsion, and grabbed his toiletry bag. Even if BSD North didn't give him privacy, he'd at least get rid of the garbage taste on his tongue.

And thanks to registering at the bar last night, at least he had a clean T-shirt for today.

Dale eased the chair out from under the doorknob, taking pains to not make noise. He didn't want Lash to think that he didn't trust him.

It wasn't that he didn't trust Lash. Not really.

Lash didn't have anything to do with it.

Teeth clean, Dale grabbed his little tablet and called up the BSD North web site. The schedule claimed a continental breakfast at eight thirty, with the keynote at nine.

Then: ten-thirty.

Dale Whitehead.

Room 102.

Wireless Networking in Derelict Urban Environments.

He stuffed the tablet into the thigh pocket of his cargo shorts, opposite his passport.

At least he wouldn't have to wait to humiliate himself. He'd be done by eleven thirty.

Dale had an hour to kill before the keynote.

He sunk into the comforting barrage of email. He'd almost finished reading dozens of messages when a new message appeared from Will, asking how last night had gone at the bar.

Dale chewed his cheek.

What to say?

I charged fifty bucks of beer, hope you're happy?

My head aches and my stomach's demanding bacon and eggs even though I ate half a damn potato farm last night?

The ShufflSoft guys gave me a commit bit and want me naked in front of the world, and that's nothing anybody needs to see?

Finally, Dale hit R to reply. *Learned things. Bought beers like you said.* He debated adding something to declare everything was fine. Instead, he sent the message and went to check his web news feed.

He'd gotten halfway through an article on next year's storage technology when someone knocked on his door.

Dale jumped like he'd been goosed.

"Hey, Dale," Lash said through the closed bedroom door. "You up?"

Dale took a deep breath. His heart hammered against his ribcage. The cozy dorm bedroom suddenly felt coffin-sized.

Lash must have heard the keyboard, and decided to be friendly.

Dale made himself stand. Two steps brought him to the door.

Swinging it open felt more difficult than lifting weights. "Hi." His tongue felt clumsy.

Lash looked impossibly chipper despite his tired features, and his voice had this annoying cheer. "I just have to set up my spare laptop, then I'll head over. You want me to show you where everything's at?"

Crap! "We need a spare laptop?"

Lash laughed. "No, I do. I've had my laptop break twice at BSD North, right before giving a talk. So I bring a spare. I set it up so it's ready, just in case." He snapped a finger. "Oh, I almost forgot! Are you the Dale Whitehead who sent in the high-loss media TCP patches?"

What, do these people memorize the whole bug database or something? "Yeah, that's me."

"Sorry I didn't recognize you before," Lash said.

"Uh, why would you?"

"That's part of the fun of these events," Lash said. "You know someone's work, but you don't really know them."

"Do you do anything with the TCP stack?" Dale said.

"No, I know better than that," Lash chuckled. "I'm storage, low-level stuff, where it hooks into VFS. And clocks, but that's kind of a sideline any more. But you came up last night, and Sergei knew who you were."

Dale hurriedly shuffled through his brain. He hadn't met a Sergei. He couldn't think of one involved in SkyBSD. "Sergei?"

"Surge," Lash said.

Dale relaxed a little. "Oh, okay." He'd interacted with the person who went by the handle of Surge, but suddenly realized he had no idea what their real name was. Or their gender.

Or, really, if Surge was human or some sort of hyper-intelligent hamster.

"He asked me to introduce you," Lash said.

Dale's neck thrummed with returned tension. "Uh, why?"

"You've sent him a whole bunch of fixes. That's part of the point of BSD cons, to meet the people you work with and talk things out. With beer."

"He's bounced a bunch of my patches back," Dale said.

"That's probably why he wants to talk," Lash said. "Sometimes a fix isn't quite right because it doesn't fit with the system as a whole. And that sort of thing is a lot easier to hash out in person." Lash studied Dale's face and narrowed his eyebrows. "It's nothing to worry about. If he didn't like your work, he'd avoid you. But five minutes with a whiteboard beats two months of emails, every time."

Dale had gone to more than one meeting with a client for exactly that reason. He willed the tension from his shoulders.

"Besides," Lash said. "Sergei is *the* man for the TCP stack. We need more people who don't just understand it, but really get how it works and how it interoperates with everything else. If a few minutes of his time can help you get that deep into it, he'd think it's totally worth it."

Dale swallowed. More attention he didn't need.

"Don't worry," Lash said. "Surge is a good guy. We did the whole CVS to Subversion conversion without killing each other."

"Uh, sure."

"Pack up your laptop," Lash said, "I'll plug my spare in, and we'll get this party started."

10

The campus hall stood three stories tall, impressively clad in pale gray-brown granite with tiny flecks of mica sparkling in the sun. The voluminous tulip beds on either side of the well-worn stair treads lofted clouds of perfume in the still air. The words *MacDonald Hall* were chiseled into a granite panel over the entryway, and a small free-standing sign circled by hostas declared the building—

"The chemistry department?" Dale said.

Lash chuckled. "Would you like to use the campus computers?"

Dale winced.

"I think the kids are using the computer hall this year," Lash continued. "We overlap them most years. All we really need are lecture halls and projectors. And there's breakfast. Coffee."

Dale perked up. "Coffee?"

"The con's coffee is terrible." Lash grinned. "I've made special arrangements for mine."

The MacDonald Hall main hall swept inward, three floors of open space soaring up to the angled skylights in the roof. The second and third floors had formal-looking mezzanines with fancy carved balusters, like they expected Parliament to move in once the ministers realized how chintzy their current digs were. A flat screen on the wall near the entrance displayed *Today's Schedule* in oversize print, supported by twin columns of names and room numbers.

The sight of the people stopped Dale as firmly as if he'd faceplanted into a brick wall.

Last night's bar crowd had nothing on the *hundreds* of people jammed in here.

Maybe half the people fit what Dale thought of as the computer nerd stereotype—a few extra pounds around the middle, thirties-to-forties, an unnaturally high percentage of them with hair cut short or entirely shaved. The other half was a mix of sci-fi con refugees, punk musicians, a few uptight business types, and a nice sprinkling of "what the *heck* is that?" Two stiffly formal Indian men, their identically-cut single-breasted suits distinguishable only by their slightly different shades of dark blue, argued intently with a bald muscular guy in a skin-tight T-shirt. Dale recognized Brian Mallard, from last night's Git discussion, lounging near open double doors at the side of the hall, greeting any number of people like they were old friends he hadn't seen for months. A heavyset woman in tight Doctor Who-themed leggings, a baggy Warcraft T-shirt, and a set of clip-on blinking red horns in her bright red hair had one hand raised as she talked to a short, skinny guy who looked almost too weak to hold his head up. Maybe his spiky bright blue hair gave his skull extra lift or something? A couple of sharply dressed Japanese men walked past, each with a steaming plastic cup in one hand. In the other hand, each held a stupidly undersized plastic plate, piled high with meticulously balanced pastries and sliced fruit.

The back of the room was absolutely filled with people, churning like piranha at the Second Annual "The Cow Fell In The River" festival. Dale glimpsed three long tables amidst them, groaning with a burden of coffee vats, heaped pastry platters, and a phalanx of steaming tureens. The fierce coffee aroma caught Dale's nose, but the rich fatty scent of bacon went down his throat and seized his stomach.

Fortunately, the crowd's tumultuous babble cloaked the rippling grumble from his gut.

Someone's probably sneezed on the Danishes already, Dale thought. *So. Many. Cooties.* Last night's carbohydrate banquet gnawed at his guilt. Still, he had to put something in his stomach so he could take his morning pills.

"Warren!" someone said. "Has your laptop blown up yet?"

Beside Dale, Lash chuckled and turned towards the ridiculously tall newcomer. Dale took the opportunity to slip into the anonymizing crowd.

The feeding frenzy wasn't quite as erratic as Dale had first thought.

Be good. Coffee. Bacon, a piece is okay. If they've got eggs, okay. No Danish, no toast. No carbs at all, or you're literally on bugs and gravel for the rest of the trip, so help me.

The two Indians joined the line behind Dale, still arguing. Dale caught a few phrases, something about the details of passing hardware access across a virtualization layer. Dale didn't know *anything* about that. He strained his ears to catch more. In the crunch of the buffet line, though, too many conversations fractured around him for Dale to really follow any one of them, no matter how interesting.

The closeness of the crowd made Dale feel caged. Trapped.

He craned his neck to peer through the crowd, and caught sight of one of the nearby doors.

No key card reader. The round handle had a jagged slit for a traditional key. Dale could hack a key lock, the cheap ones at least, but he had to do it in meatspace, and everyone would see it.

The only place to run? Straight out the front door.

And if he did that, he'd run all the way back to Detroit.

Dale focused on his breathing. Empty the lungs. All the way. Refill them, up to the top. Just like the doc told him to.

Someone bumped his overstuffed backpack.

Dale's heart pattered.

Would running all the way home be such a bad thing?

No, he was not going to freak out. It was just a buffet line.

Suddenly the stocky man in front of Dale stiffened. He glanced back at Dale, then turned sideways to face him and said in a somewhat-British accent, "How are you this morning?"

A hint of alarm tickled Dale's spine. The guy seemed nervous—had Dale done something? "I'm okay?"

"Name's Max Reinholt." He had short-cropped bleached-out hair above a sharp-angled face that looked like it had been carved from ancient oak, with axes. His pale linen sport coat looked incongruous over a T-shirt sporting a CoreBSD wireframe daemon.

"Dale. Dale Whitehead."

The crowd shuffled forward. Reinholt stepped sideways with it and glanced around Dale. "Dale, right, sorry. I haven't seen you at BSD North before."

"First time." Dale realized he wasn't the problem. Something behind him worried Reinholt. Possibilities flashed through his mind—a stalker? Angry ex-wife with a gun? No, this was Canada, they didn't have guns so she'd have what, an angry moose? No, all that was foolish.

But he still fought the urge to look over his shoulder.

Reinholt must have seen Dale twitch. "It's okay, don't look. I just—I can't talk to that man before coffee. A lot of coffee. I just flew in from Malaysia. Twelve hour jet lag."

"I get that." Reinholt's exhausted distress broke Dale's own tension. Dale suddenly had a job to do. "I can beard for you."

"Donner's not really a… a *bad* guy," Reinholt said. "He writes a bunch of BSD books. But just because I wrote the one on the CoreBSD mail server, he's always on me about doing one on the packet filter."

"People might like that," Dale said.

Reinholt shook his head. "The email book was enough work. I can't see doing another. But Donner's…" He wrinkled his nose. "He keeps telling me if I don't he will, and doesn't listen when I say *yes please*." Reinholt shook his head as if to knock an annoying insect away. "What do you think of BSD North so far?"

What am I supposed to say? We haven't even had the keynote yet. "Lots of beer," Dale said.

Reinholt snorted. "Yes, yes. We have Bob doing the keynote this year. He always does well."

"Bob?"

"Bob Matheson."

Dale scrambled through his memory. "Wasn't he—didn't he do a bunch of the BSD stuff back at Berkley?"

"Most of the network stack," Reinholt said, shuffling forward. They were almost close enough to one of the side tables to grab plates, but the line ground to a halt in front of them. "And the device driver infrastructure. He's pretty much the godfather of BSD."

"Oh, cool."

"He's here most years," Reinholt said.

Someone bumped into Dale's backpack again. He pivoted his head to try to look, but couldn't quite see. And he hadn't emptied the unneeded cables and connectors from his overburdened pack, so if he turned to look the pack would probably bludgeon someone off their feet. It's okay, he told himself. Don't worry about the crowd—think of something to say. "Does he always do the keynote?"

"Usually they bring someone in," Reinholt said. "I guess it's for the fifteenth BSD North, or something like that."

Dale fumbled for something to say. *When in doubt, ask questions. Get people to talk about themselves.* "What's the best part of the con?" Dale said.

The crowd shifted, letting Dale pluck one of the tiny plates from the dwindling stack.

Reinholt shifted back a step, moving to the other side of the table. "The hallway track. Between the talks, the dorm lounge, the bar, all of that." He looked forward to the line ahead.

Let the conversation die? Talk across the table as they picked up food? Reinholt seemed to be focused on getting breakfast, so Dale decided to do the same. A few battered slices of melon and knocked-about strawberries sat on a tray ahead, with bright yellow bananas beside them. A blueberry muffin Tower of Hanoi stood just behind them, each muffin the size of a grapefruit.

That crunchy crumble topping on the muffin looked delicious. Dale could imagine the sweetness—

No.

Dale loaded his plate with a melon slice and a banana, adding a scoop of questionably scrambled eggs. Two slices of bacon, but they were small, so really they should only count as one. He felt inordinately proud of himself, and embarrassed by that pride, as he followed the ooze of the crowd through the double doors into the cavernous lecture hall.

He'd barely gotten through the doors when the overhead speakers popped. "Find a place, people. Let's get started."

11

The lecture hall rose up before Dale in stadium tiers. Not a football stadium, but more like an old medical demonstration theater. Each tier had a long counter to serve as a desk and uncomfortable-looking swing-out plastic chairs mounted every few feet behind it. Right in front of Dale, a knot of people clustered around the podium and the lowest tier. The place smelled of too many nerdy men who had traveled too far and claimed too much breakfast.

The sudden tidal wave of noise, people excitedly arguing and greeting one another, pounded against Dale's brain.

His feet lurched to a halt.

Thick crowd, no visible aisle—how could he get through?

Someone bumped his back.

Dale's coffee threatened to slosh over the Styrofoam cup.

He felt his face flush with embarrassment.

"Come on," someone behind him said.

There! Up against the wall, someone disappeared behind the crowd.

The overhead popped again. "Places, people. Starting on time means lunch on time. Lots to do."

Dale squeezed through a tiny rivulet between knots of people to discover a broad aisle up into the stadium seats. Most the seats were already taken, either with people or with laptops left as placeholders, but Dale spied a seat in the middle of the left side. It was still empty by the time he got up that high, and with mumbled apologies he balanced his coffee, plate, and backpack so he could slip behind other attendees and claim the spot.

He set the coffee and tiny breakfast plate down on the table, lowered his bag with a huff, and squeezed himself behind the desk. The uncomfortably hard plastic chair groaned with his weight.

Aren't you glad you skipped that muffin now?

The ridiculously skinny college kid in jeans and a T-shirt sitting next to Dale hoisted his muffin off his plate and chomped it. Dale grimaced, swallowing his envy, and made himself look forward.

By the time he'd gotten his laptop plugged in, the crowd had poured into chairs. The holdouts knotted around the middle arc of the front row of chairs, but even they had started to break up.

Lash had somehow gotten a front row seat, right near the center. By another miracle, he'd gotten his hands on a tall brown cup of actual Tim Horton's coffee. The lid was gone, and steam haloed his head as he waved at the stocky man standing in front of him, obviously urging him to a seat. He had a cup of Tim's finest as well. So did the older guy with the droopy blond mustache, who seemed to be holding court a couple yards from the podium. He needed to remember those faces, if only to ask them where they'd gotten the coffee.

Ian Langton, the athletic-looking conference chair who'd registered Dale last night, slipped behind the podium, beneath a hanging screen big enough to display a wartime propaganda film behind columns of marching soldiers. "I'm about to start," he said into the mic. "If you're still standing, I'll just talk over you."

A chuckle rose from around Dale.

Dale wondered how Langton got the confidence to address the crowd. How he expected them to obey him.

But the knot of people dissolved, people streaming to their seats. By the time Dale fumbled his pill case from of his pack's side pocket and shook an allergy pill and a couple bright blue atomoxetine capsules out into his hand, almost everyone had a place.

No matter what, Dale had to take the stupid attention deficit disorder meds. Stimulants didn't work well for him, but atomoxetine kept the worst effects away. Without it he might leave his dorm room half-dressed, forget where he'd left his laptop, or—if he got really tired and stressed—forget how to understand English.

Again.

Langton leaned into the podium mic. "Welcome to the fifteenth BSD North."

Applause erupted.

The tumult echoing back from the high curved ceiling made Dale flinch. *Just the acoustics.* He balanced his pills on the narrow gap between his laptop's "enter" key and the number pad and added his applause to the end.

Langton held a couple beats to let the roar die down. "This year, we've upped the program to four tracks of programming. But I know the question most of you want answered. What you've been waiting for. Who, you wonder, will be the charity for the closing auction?"

Someone shouted, "Are you going to auction off your shirt again?"

The ends of Langton's lips twitched in a hint of a smile. "If someone'll buy it for charity, sure."

A few people laughed.

Someone behind Dale shouted, "Fifty bucks to keep your shirt on!"

More people laughed.

Langton raised a hand. "Settle down, folks. This year, we're going to pick a charity by vote. You'll need your conference badge to get a ballot. We've got the Hull Men's Mission, the Grace Hopper Conference, and, as something new, the Byward University Student Support fund. There's also a space for write-ins, so if you can build support for your cause by lunch tomorrow, you might win."

"Send Deck elk hunting!" someone called from the far side of the room.

A flash of laughter rippled through the room.

The constant interruptions grated on Dale's nerves. Yes, computer people were famous for poor social skills—but it seemed like some of these people didn't understand even basic politeness.

Langton shrugged. "If you can get enough people to write that in, that's fine. Some people might bid even higher just to send Mister Deck far, far away."

Right in front of Langton, Lash raised his coffee in salute before slugging a mouthful down.

How did Langton stay that cool? That kind of heckling would derail Dale. But Langton had hundreds of people looking down on him, literally, and he laughed with them.

Dale sipped his own coffee. It had smelled okay, but on his tongue it degraded into road tar. How had Lash had gotten that cup of Horton's?

"Second most important thing," Langton said. "Tonight, we have the group dinner down at the Irish Arms. Yes, all of us. We've rented the whole place for the evening. Thanks to one of our sponsors, Hardcase Systems…" Langton raised a hand to the far side of the room.

A broad-shouldered man in a black T-shirt faced the crowd and waved. His tight black ponytail bobbed cheerfully.

Rude audience or not, Langton owned the crowd.

In about ninety minutes, Dale would need to stand in the front of room 102 and talk about providing network service with cheap radios mounted on crumbling buildings.

He wouldn't be half this good. A quarter.

Maybe a tenth.

"Thanks to them," Langton said, "the first hour is… open bar."

The opening applause was nothing compared to this barrage. Dale couldn't help hunching his shoulders up as if to protect his ears even as he clapped. Last night had demonstrated that paying this crew's bar tab wasn't just a line item on an expense report—it was a whole business proposal, with appendices and graphs and an estimate of how many months of sales they'd need to make up for it.

As the noise died down, Dale attacked his melon. His plastic fork couldn't slice it. The flimsy tines could barely could stab into it. He'd have to eat it like a melonsicle.

"When we started BSD North," Langton continued, "the whole BSD community was splintered. In 1993, UC Berkeley gave away a complete operating system. An operating system already used by millions. So many people had taken the Berkeley Software Distribution and built their own thing on top of it. We wanted BSD North to bring together CoreBSD, SkyBSD, OmniBSD, and all the other people building on that legacy. Looking around today, I see people from all these groups."

The banana might be better than the mealy melon. Hopefully.

But the peel felt stiff, and the slightly unripe smell wrinkled Dale's nose.

Langton said, "While we all have different approaches, and different goals, and different ways of working, the people in this room are using the Berkeley legacy of freely available and freely reusable software to build the future."

Yep, the banana was just as green as Dale feared. He put it down after one hyper-starched bite, carefully setting it in the peel to keep the table clean, and attacked the bacon he'd intended as dessert.

"We have our disagreements," Langton said. "Some are philosophical. Some are technical. But we're building companies and supporting our families." Passion leaked into his voice. "And with the BSD license, we're raising the bar for software quality across the world. Projects like DrunkenSSL are making the Internet less dangerous."

How could bacon be both too crisp and too soggy?

Food or not, he had to take his pills. Last thing he needed was an ADD breakdown during his talk. Dale grimaced and made himself wash down the atomoxetine capsules with road tar—er, coffee.

Tongue poisoned with bitter glue, he checked an online map for the nearest Tim Horton's. Half a mile away on foot. Further by car.

How could any place in Canada be half a mile from a Tim Horton's?

"BSD started the Internet," Langton said. "And by coming together, by talking to each other, through cooperation and sharing, we're going to achieve wonderful things."

In the front row, right in front of Langton, Warren Lash lurched to stand.

No, he wasn't standing.

He'd straightened out in his seat.

One hand flung out, hurling a half-eaten Danish.

His empty coffee cup toppled to the floor.

Langton stopped and stared at Lash, clearly confused.

A fresh kind of fear bubbled up Dale's spine.

Lash's face bloomed a ripe tomato red.

He released a harsh, gurgling cry and collapsed across his fancy little laptop.

One arm twitched.

Then he lay still.

12

The auditorium exploded.

People leapt to their feet, some craning to see Lash's prone form, others plowing through the cramped rows to get to the aisles. The sudden smell of sick fear cut through the fug of tired travelers and mediocre breakfast.

Driven by the sudden hammering of Dale's pulse, his hands clenched into clumsy fists.

Dale knew *exactly* what made someone turn that color red.

He'd read any number of murder mysteries where killers used cyanide.

Fresh sweat exploded down his spine. His legs tensed, the flight-or-flight reflex kicking in.

Ridiculous. Lash must have keeled over from something else. Something natural. Like a stroke or an appendix or something.

A cluster of people grew at the front of the auditorium, obscuring Lash's slumped figure. Someone raised a hand.

The skinny kid next to Dale leaned over and said something, but the clamor of everyone around them drowned the kid's words.

Dale shook his head and shrugged through the shivers wracking his shoulders.

The overhead speakers crackled. "People!" Langton wasn't quite shouting, but the amplified announcement still stabbed through the uproar. "Tom Wemm is calling the ambulance right now. Steve and Rob are helping Warren, give them some room."

Five hundred voices went from shouting to whispering.

Langton said "It's probably best if everyone leaves the room. Use the rear exits. Go back to the lobby. Leave an aisle for the ambulance. Rear exits, everyone. Keep the noise down, give Steve and Rob time to work."

That nasty voice inside Dale's head whispered *Nobody can help Lash.*

But at least you won't have to share the shower any more.

Dale squashed the thought. The shower didn't matter right now. He'd happily—well, *willingly*—share the shower if it meant Lash got back up.

Maybe the poor bastard had an undiagnosed seizure condition.

He might be destined for the hospital.

Dale tried to tell himself that. Maybe Lash would spend the conference in the hospital. Get some medication for whatever had done him in and get sent home, good as new.

Lash spending a night in the hospital wouldn't be too bad. Dale would get his own shower then.

Or two nights, maybe. Just until I'm gone.

The thought embarrassed Dale even as it relieved him. The relief embarrassed him further.

The skinny kid poked Dale's shoulder.

Dale snapped back to himself with a jerk. The kid had folded his laptop and stuffed it into a tiny plaid shoulder bag, and was looking at Dale expectantly.

Right—Langton had asked them to leave the room.

And Dale was in the way. As usual.

Dale clumsily slapped his laptop lid shut and unknotted his hands enough to tug the power cord free. He tried twice to coil the cord around one hand, but wound up only creating a wad. Grimacing, Dale stuffed the knotted cord into his bag, slid the laptop into its thickly padded compartment, yanked the zippers closed, and slid both straps of the heavy bag over his left shoulder.

The mass of people oozing up the stairs resembled an audience leaving a disappointing rock concert—some excited, some talking back and forth about what had happened, some somber. The crowd squeezed into a switchback staircase barely wider than Dale's shoulders.

After the claustrophobic staircase, the windowless corridor behind the lecture hall felt open and airy. Dale's brain wobbled in his skull, and his pulse seemed to make his whole body throb.

You're being a drama king, Dale. Stop it.

Rather than following the crowd to the front hall, he staggered to the far wall and rested one hand on the wall.

Lots of things can make people turn that color. You're reading too much Agatha Christie.

Dale tried to pull in a deep breath, but his chest already seemed full.

Okay, turning that bright red can be a symptom, sure. That doesn't mean someone really poisoned Lash.

13

"Hey man, you okay?"

Standing at the edge of the hallway, Dale still couldn't catch his breath. A few feet away, people still streamed past, headed towards the grand entrance hall where they'd eaten breakfast. The babble had thinned, mostly because the narrow staircase from the conference room to this broad corridor had choked everyone down to single file. The stink of his own sweat filled Dale's nose and bile burned the back of his throat, making his swirling head even more nauseating. Without a hand on the cool concrete wall, he might have toppled over.

Someone poisoned Lash.

Ridiculous.

"Come on," someone said. "Sit down."

Dale made himself look.

It was the skinny kid who'd been sitting next to him in the auditorium. Not so much a kid, actually. Yeah, he was weirdly thin, built like a teenager and his short black hair had enough gel to stand straight as a bristle brush, but his face had a few age lines, and that Dead Kennedys T-shirt looked old enough to be legit. He had a bunch of one-inch buttons pinned to the strap of his shoulder bag— Legendary Pink Dots, Skinny Puppy, Einstürzende Neubauten, a bunch of symbols and names Dale didn't recognize but were probably also bands.

I met him last night at dinner. What was his name? Mayonnaise? No, but something like that.

"Come on," the kid—no, *man*—said. "There's a seat back here."

"I'm fine," Dale wheezed. *God, this is embarrassing.*

"'Course you are. So keep me company, I need to chill a minute after that."

Dale let the man lead him a couple yards away from the front hall, where a long low wooden bench seat had been built into the corridor wall, beneath convenient reading lights. He sagged into the bench, head still spinning, trying and failing to catch a deep breath.

"You gotta exhale before you can inhale," the man said, sinking to the bench himself.

An iron band circled Dale's chest, paralyzing his lungs.

"Breathe out," the man said. "It's okay, they've called an ambulance and they'll take care of him 'cause he's gonna be just fine. Just breathe. All the way out."

Not if he's that color.

Unsure if the heat in his face was oxygen deprivation, panic, or humiliation, Dale concentrated on his chest. His lungs. Rather than gulp for more air, he tried to tighten his chest. Everything in him screamed for more air, but instead he pushed as much as he could out.

"There you go," the man said.

He should have stayed home.

He should have never mentioned this conference to Will.

He should have been a janitor.

No, janitors probably found dead bodies more often.

But at least he could breathe again.

"I'm Jason Hellman."

That's right! "Dale Whitehead."

"Poor Lash."

Dale nodded. "Yeah."

"His heart must have given out or something."

"Cyanide." The word popped out of Dale's mouth. His stomach tightened with the urge to suck it back in.

Hellman's eyebrows went up. "Cyanide? Why would you think that?"

"That really bright red he turned," Dale mumbled.

Hellman dropped his voice. "You really think someone brought cyanide to the con?"

Dale shrugged, wishing he hadn't said anything. *You are* such *a drama king.*

"We are in the chemistry building," Hellman said. "But cyanide tastes like almonds. He'd notice that."

Bitter almonds, whatever that meant. Dale always wondered how people had figured that out. Had some Victorian chemist announced *For my next trick, I'm going to chew this sub-lethal dose of cyanide so I can tell you what it tastes like.* Or had they just sniffed a bottle of cyanide? Was cyanide vapor lethal? Did you need to wear a respirator to work in the cyanide factory?

"Maybe Lash thought it was an amaretto Danish," Hellman said.

"Amaretto? Isn't that cherry?"

"It is?" Hellman frowned. "What's the fancy word for almondish?"

"Uh… is there one?" Dale said.

"Cyanide, I guess," Hellman said. "Cyanide Danish."

"Forget I said anything," Dale said. "I'm—I'm being stupid. He probably choked."

"No, now you've got me wondering," Hellman said. He scooted to the front of the bench and hopped down. "Let's check this out."

"How?" Dale said.

"Come on, I'll show you."

14

Dale and Hellman's footsteps echoed so loudly in MacDonald Hall's vacant concrete halls that they could have found their way by echolocation. Occasional display boards choked with years of staples softened the sound, but as they hiked further from the front hall the conference attendees' conversations faded into oblivion. Gentle panels of light in the ceiling cast wavering reflections across the tile. Somewhere a floor scrubber growled, thickening the air with fresh wax.

Dale found walking a relief. The simple act of taking one step after another, passing identical doors and lecture halls, gave him a comforting illusion of progress. "Where are we going?"

"I did a couple years here," Hellman said, leading Dale up a hollow stairwell. His face might claim he had age, but he bounced up like a teenager. "Chem was one of my favorite subjects. Well, that and girls, of course. And drinking. I aced drinking, you know. And girls. Back in the day, the department was just getting computers." The sound of the floor stripper grew louder as they approached the second floor, making Hellman raise his voice. "I turned out to be really good at the computers, good enough that some of the grad students paid me to write software to solve their problems. Then the profs, and before I knew it, I was too busy making money programming to go to class. It never let up. But good old BU is traditional, they never change anything." The floor scrubber's roar drowned out anything else he might have said.

Hellman's small stature didn't affect his ability to climb stairs. He almost pranced up. They shot up past the second floor, where the stink of liquid wax through the glass door became a stench so strong it seemed to set in Dale's huffing lungs. Hellman kept going, straight up to the third floor.

"Back in the day," Hellman continued as if the floor waxer hadn't interrupted, "the big prize in the department was access to the chemical storage. The faculty only hired the students that they really liked, and they had to account for everything. They didn't want students, like, licking the lead foil or making thermite. Professor Habrasanian said he wanted me to work there once I hit my third year, but then he hired me to write code my second year, and, well, I never made it that far. Thermite's pretty cool, though. Impresses the ladies, 'specially when it's really cold out and you take her ice fishing but don't want to get all sweaty cutting a hole. Here we go."

The other doors in Macdonald Hall were suggestions, but these looming metal portcullises were commands. The hinges were hidden, the bolt protected by a plate, the lock a sturdy industrial model. If you wanted to keep mischievous students with more brains than sense out of the stocks, you'd need doors like this.

A printed sign taped to one of the doors said *CLOSED UNTIL 18 AUGUST.*

"See?" Hellman said. "You'd need a prof to get in there right now, and they're all out for the summer. Or Public Safety, they could do it too."

"You're right." The climb had left Dale a little breathless, but the implacable doors soothed him. Where would people get cyanide these days, anyway? Today wasn't like back in 1920s, when every household had poisons lying around in medicines and cleaners and who knew what. Today, poisoning someone meant bug killer or drain declogger.

"Of course I'm right," Hellman said. He thumped one of the doors, right above the locking knob, with the heel of his hand. "Nobody's getting—"

The door clicked.

Rocking from Hellman's blow, the door eased open half an inch.

15

Dale's stomach plunged.

Hellman immediately fell silent, jaw hanging open.

The door to the chemical stores swung less than an inch, but it might as well have swung wide and exposed a portal into deep space or Dinosaur Land.

Adrenaline thrummed in Dale's veins. The stink of floor wax clotted in his nose. His heavy backpack dragged his shoulder like an anchor.

"Christ!" Hellman said. "What the hell?" He reached for the doorknob.

"Don't!" Dale said.

Hellman froze.

"Fingerprints," Dale said. The scurry up the stairs had warmed his muscles, but he shivered anyway. Heat blossomed between his spine and his heavy laptop backpack.

Hellman looked at Dale incredulously, then nodded. "Right. So…" He waved his hand back and forth over the door.

The vacant hall suddenly seemed to loom around them, all the doors leading to laboratories and classrooms threatening to disgorge a professor or a police officer who would dash up and shout *Aha! Breaking into the cyanide store again, are we?*

Dale licked his lips and willed his stomach to settle. "We've got to tell someone."

"They'll think we did it," Hellman said, his voice a whispered hiss.

"We were with each other."

"I had my seat," Hellman whispered, "but nobody pays attention to me. I saw you coming up the stairs, but I can't really say I noticed you before that. I mean, you could have slipped something to him before I got there. I don't think you did, but they'll think it, that's what cops do."

"This is not an Agatha Christie novel," Dale said, trying to make himself sound certain.

"No, it's not," Hellman said. "People go to jail here even if they're innocent. You don't know what the cops are like here, they'll come down on you like a falling server rack even though you ain't done nothing."

"This is Canada," Dale said. "They're not that bad up here."

"I went to school here!" Hellman hissed. "You've got no idea. Something innocent, they'll be all over you."

"Maybe it's coincidence?" That sounded even weaker than Dale thought. "Here, move over a minute."

"You're not going in there!" Hellman said. "You were the one who brought up fingerprints. If you're right, if he was poisoned, they'll be up here right away with the dusting kits and dogs and infrared and all that stuff."

"I just want to look at the door," Dale said.

Hellman retreated a shallow step. "Just don't touch it."

"I'm not going to touch it." Dale lowered himself to one knee, clumsy with the backpack. He really needed to clean that monster bag out when he got home. Strip it down to what he actually needed on a day-to-day basis, not every tool he ever needed. His knee ached on the cool smooth tile, but it brought him face-to-face with the door knob.

And the lock.

The stainless steel lock didn't have a brand name engraved in it, meaning that the manufacturer felt no need to advertise. The lock was either great, or terrible. The heavy knob had been in place for long enough that countless greasy hands had softened the metal's shine and given it a faint patina.

Dale squinted, hope and worry tangled in his head.

Worry won. "Crap."

"What is it?" Hellman said, his voice rising above a whisper. He seemed ready to break from tension.

"The lock," Dale said. "There's scratches all around it. Bright ones. Either someone had a really hard time getting their key in today, or someone had a really hard time picking it."

Hellman looked down, as if he could see through the floor all the way to the conference hall two levels down. Dale could read the thoughts on his face. *The lock was picked. The conference is the only event in the building.* "But—lock picking is maybe the most common hacker hobby. Not like video games, but still."

Dale peered at the network of fine scratches around the lock. "They had a real problem picking this one. It looks like a pretty good lock."

Hellman gave a tiny, almost hysterical giggle. "Maybe they're a lousy picklock. Could be that."

"No, it's a good lock," Dale said.

"You pick locks?"

"I used to." Dale heaved himself upright. His chest still felt tight, but the worst of the panic had faded to a simmering unease. "We've got to say something. They'll find out anyway."

"I'm not saying a thing," Hellman said defiantly.

"Look!" Dale snapped, glaring down at Hellman. "They *will* find out. They always do. It's better to tell the truth than make them dig for it."

"They've got nothing to tie us to here," Hellman said. "Far as anyone knows, we went out the back for a smoke."

"Do you smoke?"

"Not any more—but that's not the point."

Dale said, "You keep your mouth shut and the cops find out you were up here and ask why, what are you going to say?"

"They won't figure out we've been here!"

Dale threw up a hand. "Dude, you smacked the door! That's your handprint on there."

Hellman looked at the door and grabbed the bottom of his shirt, like he was ready to whip it off and polish the wood.

"And how many people saw us walk up here?" Dale said.

Hellman froze.

"And I'm a terrible liar," Dale said. "Really awful. If someone asks me if I was up here and I say no, they'll see it straight off."

"Nobody's that terrible," Hellman said.

"I am."

"Oh yeah?" Hellman snorted. "When was the last time you got laid?"

Dale leaned back, feeling new warmth climbing up his neck. "That's none of your business."

"Wow," Hellman said. "That long? You *are* a terrible liar." He stared at the wall. "Look—just leave me out of it."

"How? I mean, would I have found this without you?"

"I don't know! Just…" Clearly overflowing with frustration, Hellman smacked the door with his palm again.

The door shot back into place.

Click.

And stayed shut.

"Did you lock it?" Dale said.

"I…"

"They left it unlocked." Dale strained to keep his voice from rising to a shout, transforming it to an aggrieved whisper. "You just tampered with evidence!"

"Shit!" Hellman danced back.

"It'll be okay," Dale said. "Don't freak out."

"I'm not freaking out!" Hellman said, glancing up and down the empty hall.

"That's what I said earlier."

"I better go," Hellman said.

"Hang on a moment."

"Look!" Hellman snapped. "The cops know who I am, okay? I barely got off last time. If they think I'm part of this, I am totally screwed."

"What?" Dale said. "They think you killed someone?" Somehow, switching into the more reasonable role soothed his stomach.

"No!" Hellman shouted. He gritted his teeth and dropped back to a whisper. "Possession. Not much, just enough."

Dale rolled his eyes. "This is Canada, they don't care."

"I'm from Canada," Hellman said. "They care a lot. They just won't shoot me for it."

"It's a different thing," Dale said. "I mean—what, weed? A few ounces? That's a whole different thing than, than…" He waved a hand at the closed door. "This."

"One more and I'm in jail," Hellman said.

"And withholding evidence?" Dale said. "You think that'll look better?"

Hellman shook his head, casting around like a snared animal.

"Look," Dale said, "You wanted to show me I was overreacting, so we walked up together."

Hellman's head still shook, but more slowly.

"You're innocent. I trapped you in your spot, remember? And I'm the one who freaked out that he'd been poisoned. You're just, just an innocent bystander, who wanted to show me it was a crazy idea."

Hellman inhaled through his teeth. "Right. You're right."

"So let me do the talking."

Hellman shook his head. "You're… this can't…"

"It'll be okay."

"Do you even know *how* to talk to cops?"

Dale gave his first honest smile of the day. "I'm from Detroit."

16

But there weren't any police to talk to.

Dale forced himself to march back downstairs, a hollow façade of confidence on his face and Hellman trailing in his wake. The BSD North crowd filled the spectacular entry hall, with a few tight knots of people up on the second and third floor mezzanines. Unlike an hour ago, the whole crowd looked subdued. People leaned their heads together to speak quietly, eyes glancing side to side. Even the four women cleaning away the devastated buffet dishes worked soberly.

A clear path led from the conference room doors to the MacDonald Hall entrance. Through the glass doors, Dale glimpsed an ambulance pulling away, lights flashing.

The quiet voices and turned-away eyes suited a close brush with death. But Dale couldn't help thinking of the unlocked chemical supply closet and Lash's fire-engine red face. Those quiet glances and muted murmurs were perfectly appropriate for *I can't believe he's dead.*

But if someone wanted to mutter *our cunning plan worked* to a conspirator, they'd look like that too.

"No cops," Hellman mumbled. "Don't tell me you're going to the police station."

"There's got to be one," Dale hissed. "They always show up when this happens." He couldn't help glancing to either side for eavesdroppers, but everyone looked insulated in their own private conversations.

"Maybe he's not dead," Hellman said. "He might've had a fit. Or a gall bladder attack. That happens."

"Sure." Dale raised his head to scan through the crowd, peering through the narrow gaps to the people beyond. He glimpsed royal blue and said, "There!"

"Where?"

"An officer. By the front door."

"There's only one?" Hellman said. "He's busy. Don't bother him."

Dale turned to slip between clumps of people. "I'll wait my turn."

"Dammit," Hellman growled.

But he followed.

The officer, a woman in a stiffly starched Ottawa Police uniform, stood with conference chair Langton. Langton stood with his spine straight, as if deliberately holding himself upright, but his shoulders slumped almost as much as his face. Despite the crowd in the entry hall, several feet of empty air surrounded the pair. Dale hesitated at the invisible barrier, fighting the urge to fade back, then with a conscious effort lurched forward to violate that gap.

"—just a moment before," Langton said. "I don't get it."

"These things happen," the officer said. "Every year or so, we get a stroke or a heart attack at one of these events. It's always a shock, sure. But there's nothing you could have done."

"But," Langton said. "But, if someone was going to die of a heart attack, it wouldn't be Warren. We've got folks a lot less healthy than him."

Like me, Dale thought.

"You never know." The officer shook her head. "You just never know."

Langton's twitching efforts to keep his face calm only trumpeted his distress.

Standing in the empty ring around the two, Dale felt uncertain. He had to say something—but the officer and Langton were an island of conversation, as intimate as if they sat at a table for two. Dale couldn't see how to drag up the metaphorical third chair without being a jerk. Just break in? Step in between and blurt out that someone had picked the lock on the chemistry supply closet?

"The important thing," the officer said, "is that you keep your crowd here under control. Nothing's definite. The paramedics might still be able to do something for your friend. I'll see you're notified as soon as we know anything."

"Thanks," Langton said. His eyes roamed the crowd sightlessly.

Dale caught himself nervously licking his lip. Was this the time to jump in? Was their conversation done? It sounded like it, almost, but Langton wore this hesitant, lost expression as his gaze brushed the crowd. The officer was still watching Langton, like she waited for a more complicated answer.

Dale tensed himself to step forward.

"Give them a little time," the officer said.

They weren't done talking! Dale's heart lurched, but he managed to smother the step into a twitch.

The officer continued, "Then call people back in. Tell them we'll send any news as soon as we have it. If you have any trouble, call the campus station. I'll try to stay around this part of campus just in case."

"Okay," Langton said. "I'll do that. Any idea when we'll know?"

"Nope," the officer said. "But longer is better. They'll wait to say he's going to be fine until they know what's going on."

"Right," Langton said.

They stood silent a moment.

Dale steeled himself to speak.

"I'll tell them that," Langton said.

Dale's teeth clanged together in frustration. *For heaven's sake, I'm trying to tell you where the killer got cyanide and you're saying the victim might be okay.*

But maybe all Dale's worries were exaggerations, inflated by his own imagination. Maybe Lash hadn't really stopped breathing in front of everyone. Or perhaps the paramedics had gotten his heart started.

Maybe Lash had had a seizure.

"Hey," Langton said. "You're Warren's roommate, aren't you?"

Dale came to himself with a jerk. Langton's eyes were focused on his face. "Uh—y—yeah."

"Oh, good," the police officer said. "I need to speak with you. I'm Officer Senese." Her pale, freckled face looked open and direct. Even sympathetic.

Dale nodded.

"What's your name?" Senese said.

"Dale. Dale Whitehead."

Senese raised a notebook and concentrated on scribbling a note. "Dale. White… head. Thank you. Did Lash say anything to you about any medical issues?"

"No," Dale said.

"Anything he was concerned about?" Officer Senese said.

"No," Dale said. "Uh, we didn't talk much."

"How well did you know him?"

Not well enough to poison him, Dale thought. "We met at check-in yesterday." Surely the police couldn't suspect Dale? Already? "Uh, and we walked over today. We talked about coffee."

"He liked coffee?" Officer Senese said.

"He *needed* coffee," Dale said. "He'd flown in from Utah, or some place like that. Yesterday."

Officer Senese nodded and pursed her lips.

Dale caught himself looking at her face, not like he was having a conversation, but appreciating how her strong Native cheekbones contrasted with her freckled cheeks. *Stop it, dude. You are* not *going to hit on the police officer. Gah, you're shameless!* Dale knew perfectly well he wouldn't flirt with Senese—he never flirted, with anyone. Still, a sudden heat on his neck threatened to crawl up to his face. "That's really all I know," he said.

"Thank you, Mister Whitehead," Senese said.

How was Dale supposed to say: *he was poisoned. Cyanide.* "You're welcome."

Langton cleared his throat. "I best get people back in."

"Thank you, Mister Langton," Senese said, flipping her notebook closed. "As soon as we have word of your friend, I will let you know."

"Right."

Dale tensed. Now or never.

17

"Officer Senese!" Dale blurted. No, too loud, the whole crowd will hear that.

The police officer raised both her eyebrows. "Yes, Mister Whitehead?"

"Uh… upstairs. The supply closet. Where they keep the dangerous chemicals?" Dale paused to swallow even though his mouth felt bone-dry. "It's unlocked."

"Probably some professor working off-semester," Senese said. "Being lazy while the students are gone. But I'll take a look while I'm here."

Words boiled inside Dale. *Someone picked the lock. Took cyanide. Fed it to Lash.*

No, he'd sound like a maniac. Like one of those lunatic Internet-affirmed conspiracy theorists. "Thanks."

"Good day, gentlemen." Senese turned to go.

Langton gave Dale a distracted nod, then faded into the crowd.

Dale stood there, uncertain. He should have said more. No, he'd made the report. Stated the facts. The police could put things together on their own, back at the station. Wait—that guy was poisoned? Didn't we get a report of an unlocked chemical closet? Aha, a Clue!

He'd done the right thing.

A faint hope nibbled at his soul. Senese had sounded like Lash might be all right. Perhaps all this really was for nothing.

Hellman materialized at his elbow. He spoke just as quietly as everyone else. "Thanks, man."

Dale nodded. "We had to say something."

"Yeah, I get it."

Dale turned back towards the crowd. *Please, let me be wrong.*

The only response came from his grumbling stomach.

Bugs and gravel. Bugs and gravel.

The clock was a hair's breadth from 10:30. The thought that he needed to get ready to give his talk drifted through his mind. Dale shook his head. Nobody was heading back towards the auditorium. His talk wasn't in the auditorium, though, was it? He could check on his phone, but the fifty-inch screen on hall's brick wall bore the schedule. Dale slipped between knots of quietly talking computer geeks until he was close enough to read the text.

There he was, light blue letters on black: his name, room 102, 10:30.

The digital clock at the top of the screen silently melted over to 10:28.

Should he go find room 102? Nobody else was going anywhere, though. Would they delay his talk? He could go now and say nobody had showed up—he'd given the talk to his living room, to an audience of four apartment walls and his two gerbils, Stallone and Schwarzenegger.

Maybe they'd just cancel the first round of talks. Let him off the hook entirely.

A man is dead, and you're worried about your talk?

But he couldn't do anything about Lash. Not really.

Dale wasn't even sure the man was dead.

His stomach grumbled again, this time with acid.

Maybe that poison Danish wasn't meant for Lash. Maybe someone poisoned a random pastry, and Lash got lucky. Maybe it was an accident. Or he had a seizure.

At least Dale hadn't eaten a Danish.

You don't know anything. Take control of yourself. No freaking out.

Dale forcibly relaxed his hands. Fresh sweat soaked the T-shirt's armpits and the base of his spine, beneath the burdensome backpack. His feet already hurt, aching against the soles of his sneakers. He wasn't accustomed to traipsing around on hard tile floors. The smell of bleach from the crew cleaning the buffet tables irritated his sinuses.

Maybe he should go back into the auditorium. Take a load off. Plug in. Check his email.

Yeah, that would work. Get out of his own head for a few minutes. Wait to hear what the hospital said. Langton had told everyone to leave the room, but that was so they could get Lash out. Surely they could go back in now.

Dale ducked around a small clique of men listening to an overweight bald guy in a wickaway shirt, cargo shorts, and bright orange plastic sandals over raggedy off-white socks quietly but intensely pontificate, arms making great circling loops with each word. He saw two paths through the crowd, but one of them took him right past Pokotylo. Dale didn't feel like putting up with another random drive-by sleazing, so he turned the other way. The crowd shifted. Another knot blocked his path, half a dozen people with their heads bent tight together, but he snuck around them.

"He's dead," someone said as Dale passed.

Dale paused.

"We don't know that," another voice said.

"You don't turn that color if you're alive," the first voice said. It sounded somewhat familiar, with an accent that might be British.

Dale looked over his shoulder.

The gawky guy on the edge of a cluster of people said, "Anyone knows you turn that color from cyanide."

Dale knew that man. He'd looked at those wire-rimmed glasses just last night. He'd fixed the man's name in his memory, damn it!

Someone else gave a short coughing laugh. "You're being a drama queen, man."

The British-ish speaker caught Dale in the corner of his vision and turned his head. "Dale. How are you doing?"

Glasses, polo shirt—his name was something about a bird, a duck… "Hi," Dale said.

"You look a little pale," the man said. He wore a conference name tag around his neck, but it had flipped to expose the blank white back.

Duck, duck—Mallard! Brian Mallard! He was arguing with, with Gerry Peterson about Git last night.

Dale made himself inhale. "A little shook up, that's all."

"That's right," Mallard said. "Your first time here, isn't it?"

Dale nodded.

"Everyone, this is Dale." Mallard waved a hand at the half-dozen people standing in their cluster. "Dale, this is everyone."

Like I'm supposed to learn everyone's name that way? Dale stuffed the irritation down. Right now, even if everyone introduced themselves and offered photo ID, he'd have a terrible time remembering their names. Instead, he raised a hand with a sliver of relief. "Hello, everyone."

"Mallard, you are the worst," said the man with the bright red T-shirt. Dale felt huge, but his stomach was a pale shadow of this guy's massive beer belly. "I'm Sergei." His hand moved around the circle. "You know Brian, but this is Alex, Rob, Paul, Kris, and Amanda."

Dale eyes went from face to face. Alex—no, that was Alex, before Rob, then Kris—no, Kris was the Korean woman—no, she was Amanda. He forced himself to slow down before he lost Mallard's name. "Hi."

"Howdy," Amanda said. The Texas drawl was unique, so far. Maybe he could remember her name.

"We were just saying how Warren'll be fine," the tall skinny man in the sport jacket said. Alex? No, he was third around, that made him… Kris?

Fighting down the frustration, Dale said, "I hope you're right."

Mallard shook his head, but held silent.

Sergei said, "Are you Warren's roommate?"

"That's me."

A brilliant white grin split Sergei's face. "Great. You're just the man I wanted to see."

Dale pressed his thumb into the palm of his hand, trying to subtly ease the eruption of tension. "What for?"

"The TCP patches you sent in. Warren said you were here."

Abrupt understanding eased Dale's chest. Lash had mentioned something about this on the way over. "You must be Surge."

"That's me," Surge said with exaggerated cheer. "I wanted to talk to you about your patches. Let's go somewhere a little quieter."

Dale's heart beat with a whole new tension. If Surge accepted his work, this trip might be worthwhile.

Access to one percent of the Internet?

And he'd never be able to tell anyone.

18

Surge led Dale back down the hallway leading towards the stairs, coming to a stop by the same bench Dale had plopped down on as he left the auditorium. The cinderblock walls gleamed with fresh off-white paint, giving a slight echo to the rumble of conversation drifting from the entrance hall. The floor waxing machine had moved out of hearing, but a distant aroma of freshly polished linoleum tile still underlay the air.

"This'll work," Surge said, swinging his tiny backpack off his shoulder and plopping his bulk onto the wooden bench. He rubbed his round red face with hands like hams. "Sheesh, what a day."

"Yeah." Dale sank onto the bench, turning sideways so he didn't have to slip out of his heavy pack. Unless they were staying put for half an hour or so, getting that bag off his shoulders wasn't worth the effort of dragging it back on. "They should call to restart the conference any time now, shouldn't they?"

Surge shook his head. "Right. We don't know—" He heaved in a deep breath. "We don't know anything about Warren." He sucked down another breath.

Dale would happily talk about code, but Surge's distress left him feeling itchily uncomfortable. How did you deal with a stranger? Especially a stranger whose worst suspicions might be right? "Sure," Dale said uneasily. "He'll be fine."

Surge's voice wobbled as he said, "Oh, don't sound so confident there." He rubbed his face again. "Sorry, late night last night." He dropped his hands. "Right. Enough of that. TCP patches."

Dale's breath caught. Had Surge figured out the trickery in Dale's work? "Sure. What's up?"

"You've got some extensive changes there. I'm concerned about the fast path effects, though."

Dale let the breath out, relaxed. "I tested on our network. Everything seemed fine, but…"

"It's the but that I worry about." Surge rubbed a hand on the front of his bright red shirt, over his heart, and studied his palm like he expected to see a wound. "About a quarter of the Internet runs through the SkyBSD TCP stack. I need to be really careful about what we let in."

"Of course," Dale said. He fought to seem relaxed, but his shoulders kept wanting to hunch up and his lungs ached to hyperventilate. After months of work, bent over his keyboard until the night turned to morning, this conversation might—just *might*—be the final piece he needed.

Keep cool.

Surge said, "I'm concerned about the memory structures you use."

Dale thrummed like a ruler struck against a desk. He fought to keep his voice relaxed despite the cranking-chain tightening of his spine. "They're straight out of Knuth. You can't get much more traditional than that." Innocence, that was the key. Maybe Surge had figured out the poison pill, but Dale could pretend to be unaware of the implications.

It had seemed so easy, sitting at his desk. He'd never really expected to talk about these face-to-face.

"That's not the issue." Surge leaned against the bench back. The fluorescent lighting made the dark circles beneath his eyes more visible. "We have enough trouble getting people who can work on the TCP stack. I try to hold the hand-tuned assembler to the absolute essentials, and stick with well-known algorithms. If we add new ones, I need them to be really clear."

"Okay," Dale said cautiously. His back creaked with the effort of restraining the anticipation sparking through him. "They're textbook. How much more clear can they be?"

"The textbook's fine," Surge said. "And I could figure out why you did things that way. But that's the problem—I had to figure it out."

What?

Surge must have seen Dale's confusion. "I had to sit down and draw out the data flows. They work, but I had to work too hard."

"So… you want me to rewrite the code so it's easier to understand?" Dale's stomach knotted. He'd worked hard on those changes, developing something that improved performance without losing those subtle side effects.

"No, no, no." Surge waved a hand. "I want more comments in your code. Don't make me figure out what you're doing, just flat-out tell me."

Dale's stomach relaxed. Comments wouldn't change the functioning of the code, or the memory handling. "Yeah, I can do that."

"Put some more comments in your patches, and send them back in. Attach them to the same bug report."

"Right," Dale said.

"Having said that, though," Surge said, slipping his laptop out of his bag, "let's talk about some of the specific changes. That field you added to the media layer internal structure, for high-loss environments... can't you just make do with one of the existing error flags?"

Dale's stomach re-knotted. He didn't want anyone digging too exhaustively into his changes. Worse, he'd expected any questions to come over email, not in person. SkyBSD ran over email. "There's all kinds of loss..." he started.

Surge started grilling Dale on the code suggestions he'd submitted. The questions felt like a barrage, an avalanche of distrust. *It's not that he knows. He couldn't know. You'd have to be running ShufflSoft on top of SkyBSD to see how all this fit together.* Dale hadn't felt so gruelingly interrogated since the last time a paranoid, constipated auditor from one of the big Detroit auto firms had scrutinized Dale's network before granting the company a contract.

For every question, though, he had an answer why it was the best solution. Surge nibbled around the edges, suggesting changes here and there where Dale had overlooked something.

After only ten minutes or so, Dale's sweat drenched dark circles in his shirt. A headache throbbed with his heartbeat, and he kept tasting bitter bile at the back of his mouth. His tongue felt oversized and clumsy, unwilling to form words even though he had a decent idea what to say.

Finally, Surge leaned back. "Chill, buddy. It's not about you. You've done good work."

Dale froze. "Uh… thanks."

"Really. I'm not trying to fit you into an Iron Maiden. I'm just—the SkyBSD network stack is my responsibility. There's a lot of us, but I'm the senior person." Surge studied Dale's face. "I like your work, but I need to be absolutely sure it fits. And that you fit."

"Me?" Dale said.

Surge shrugged. "We've had people submit great work, but they turned out to be jerks. More trouble than they were worth. We're not just software—we're a community. If you keep submitting patches, though, and they're all this quality, you'll probably get a commit bit."

More exposure? "I'm not looking for a commit bit," Dale said quickly. If both the SkyBSD and Shufflsoft changes had Dale's name on them, he'd lose all deniability.

One side of Surge's mouth quirked up. "Nobody is. But you keep making improvements, and it'll be easier to give you a commit bit than pull the changes in myself." He leaned back against the bench, one huge arm resting on its back. "You make those tweaks. Lots of comments, remember. More comments than you think you need. If the patches still look good, I'll get them into the SkyBSD network test cluster. We'll see what happens under load. Okay?"

Dale let out a breath, suddenly realizing how much his ribs ached. "Okay."

"And when Warren gets out of the hospital, be sure to tell him that I had to introduce myself," Surge said, forcing levity. "He's falling down on the job."

"You known him long?" Dale said.

"Twenty years or so," Surge said. He leaned back, resting his eyes. "We did all the work to switch from CVS to Subversion. Well, he did the repo switch. I wrote a bunch of software to keep our workflow." He shook his head. "Losing Warren changes everything in SkyBSD."

Surge's lips grew tight. "Not as much as something like switching to Git would, but still."

Dale couldn't help wondering what, exactly, Lash's death would change.

And who wanted that change to happen.

19

The wooden bench slats dug into Dale's rear. He abruptly felt very aware of the corridor's atmosphere, as if the air conditioners had recycled the same air once too often. His backpack's flat back made a hollow at the base of his spine, where Dale's heat and sweat became a sauna. His mouth tasted of questionable breakfast and just a hint of coppery fear.

A few feet away, Surge heaved in a breath and rubbed his palms into his eyes.

Dale licked his lips. "You don't seem to get along too well with Lash."

Surge laughed, dropping his hands. "We have our differences, but he was basically cool." His eyebrows narrowed. "Why do you say that?"

"Wasn't that you arguing with him?" Dale asked. "In the bar."

"Oh, that." Surge waved a hand. "He's on the—the, uh, harassment committee."

"You have a committee to—" Dale stopped, face flushing. "For dealing with people who harass others? Like, Internet harassment?"

Surge rolled his eyes. "It's a new thing. He's got some stupid ideas on how the policy should work. Someone got their feelings hurt, and he's waaay overreacting. Wants to boot people out of the projects for bad manners online."

"Didn't you guys have to do that before?" Dale said.

Surge waved a hand. "Once, and he was misbehaving on the SkyBSD mailing lists. This is for Twitter and stuff—third-party sites. We don't control that, and it's not really a big problem anyway. Not enough to spend all this time and energy on, or change our whole culture."

"If it's not that big a deal, why make a committee?" Dale said.

Surge rolled his eyes. "Because Dora got in a fight with someone online, and she's making a great big fuss about it. A few web sites picked up the story, and now it's a public relations mess."

Dale had heard the story months ago. He hadn't been terribly interested then, at least not interested enough to go digging into it. People had been flinging mud on each other on the Internet since the earliest days. At some level, he was surprised that the first message transmitted on the Net hadn't been an F-bomb. He opened his mouth to say so, but Surge rolled over him. "I mean, this is the Internet. You need to have a thick skin. If it was news any time someone dogpiled on Twitter or got called a string of four-letter words on IRC, there wouldn't be anyone *on* the Net. And Warren wanted to make rules that required everyone with a commit bit be polite to each other everywhere."

Dale frowned. "Is polite so bad?"

"Polite is fine," Surge said. "But what about freedom of speech? And if someone's being a dick, or you're just goofing around, what then? I don't want a good developer getting their access yanked just because they got in a tit-for-tat with some chick."

Dale grimaced. Surge's argument sounded okay, up until that last word. How could he say so without pissing Surge off?

No. This isn't your fight. Get your patches in. Remember your real goal.

Dale eased the breath back out, stretching the silence. "So… when do you want them? The updated patches?"

"Now is good," Surge said. "Make some comments during dead time."

"Dead time?" Dale glanced back up the hall.

"You know," Surge said, leaning closer. "Not all the talks are great. You find out that you're in a dud, take the time and add your comments. You have any trouble, hit me up on IRC. Are you on the con channel?"

"There's a con channel?" Dale said.

"It's 'BSD North,' one word, on EFNet," Surge said. "I'll be there. And people make groups for dinner tonight."

At the mention of dinner, Dale's stomach didn't merely growl. It roared.

"I'll let you know if there's any problems," Dale said quickly, trying to cover it up. *Shut up!* Dale tried to keep the sudden warmth from his face. How could he be hungry after this morning? *You get bugs and gravel, dude. Keep it up, I'll take away the gravel.*

"Cool."

The noise from the front room swelled, voices rising like someone turned the volume up. Dale glanced over his shoulder to see the conference crowd shifting, the quiet circles draining to one side.

"Looks like we're starting back up," Surge said. "Shall we?"

"Sure."

"This time," Surge said, "maybe we can get more than five minutes into the opening ceremony before someone drops dead."

20

The churning mass of computer nerds felt much less energized as they shuffled up into the arcs of auditorium seats. Where they'd been all noisy excitement at breakfast, Lash's death—*hospitalization, that's all we know right now, he's in the hospital*—had drained the joy from the gathering. The room stank of bleach and soap, where the cleaning crew had attacked Warren's spilled coffee.

That was evidence, Dale thought, looking at the gleaming tiles. *They threw away his breakfast, his coffee, everything. How are the police supposed to find any clues now?*

The answer was, they wouldn't.

Dale let that grim thought gnaw at him as he trudged up the stairs, letting it bulldoze over the itch of the crowd around him. It worked, up until the moment he got near the back of the room and saw a scrawny geezer in a painfully formal button-down shirt and tie planted in the chair he'd vacated.

He took my spot! Dale's outrage flashed, and just as quickly vanished. The conference didn't have assigned seating.

"Seats, people!" Langton called from the podium. "We need to get started."

Dale glanced around. The row he'd sat in—full, like the row in front of it. An empty seat in the row behind it, right up against the wall—no, that refugee from a seventies punk band was weaseling through the aisle to it now. He knew it was irrational, but dread at being left without a seat, or worse—standing there while everybody else found a seat, then the crowd pointing out the last free spot, front row center, where everybody could see him slink into position, knotted his stomach.

Maybe Lash's seat would be empty.

No, there—in the middle of the center section, where he'd have to squeeze past half a dozen occupied spots, but in the rear. Dale hopped up a row and muttered "Excuse me" to the gray-haired woman sitting at the end. She didn't even look at him, just squeezed forward without taking her eyes from her screen.

Pulse thudding in his ears, he plopped into the empty chair just as Langton shouted, "Okay, some announcements. We're behind, so I'll make this real short."

Langton looked like he'd run a marathon in the last hour. His eyes had grown dark circles, and his shoulders slumped with the weight of his worries. Sweat gleamed on his scalp as he said, "I haven't heard from the hospital yet, but I'm sure Warren's fine. Unfortunately, we're behind schedule. You might have noticed our first round of talks are supposed to be going on right now."

Dale's ears perked, and he paused in plugging in his laptop. Yes, he was close to getting his code changes accepted—but he still had a talk to give.

"I've talked to the committee, and to a few other folks. This is what we're going to do." Langton licked his lips. "Tomorrow, we're knocking five minutes off of each break, taking them down to ten minutes each. Tomorrow's lunch will be one hour instead of ninety minutes. All together, that gives us an extra fifty minutes for talks. We're shifting the start time tomorrow from ten AM to nine thirty."

The wildly bearded man on Dale's left groaned loudly, but not loudly enough to drown out the chorus of similar groans from around the lecture hall.

"I know," Langton said, "but we had people come here to see these talks, and to give them. You'll have to knock off drinking half an hour earlier, or show up with thirty extra minutes of hangover."

Tomorrow morning. Dale let out a breath.

He'd psyched himself up to present his paper this morning. Putting it off relaxed him, but left a constant itch of undone work in the back of his brain. From a lifetime inside his own mind, he knew that itch would be a constant irritation until he completed the job.

Can't worry about it now. There's nothing to do.

"This is our fifteenth year," Langton said. "So, without further interruption, let's have our keynote." Langton raised a hand towards the side. "For those new to the BSD community, allow me to introduce someone who's been around so long, today's community formed around him. Someone who helped me put together BSD North. The one, the only, Bob Matheson." Langton clapped as he stepped aside, sparking polite applause from the crowd.

Dale had seen Matheson in the Royal Oak the night before: a scrawny-looking guy with an absurdly oversized, drooping gray mustache. He wore a button-down shirt, navy blue tie, and black slacks straight out of the 1950s IBM Corporate Dress manual, his thinning blond hair combed straight back from his high forehead. He looked around the lecture hall with the distracted air of someone trying to solve two hard problems at once. "Hello."

Reinholt had called Matheson the godfather of BSD, but he didn't look like the order-a-hit sort of godfather. More the boringly reliable sort who gave you money for your tenth birthday and advised you to invest it.

Dale had to concentrate on his typing to enter his cumbersome password correctly, but as Matheson spoke Dale quickly recognized the flat, detached tone. He'd heard that Matheson was a good speaker, but the man's mind clearly wasn't on his talk today.

Not really surprising, was it?

By tomorrow morning, when Dale gave his talk, they'd know if something had happened to Lash—no. They would hear if Lash was still alive.

It was the uncertainty that drained the life from Matheson's voice.

That voice threatened to drain the life out of Dale.

Dale tightened his lips and called up one of the patches he'd discussed with Surge. They wanted comments? He could add comments while keeping half an ear on the presentation.

But as always, once he started thinking about a computing problem, Dale sank into an ocean of code and left the air of the real world behind.

21

The lecture hall chairs were meant for college students. Not the "hey I'll go back to school" sort, either, but kids who'd just escaped high school and still had the slenderness of youth. The hard plastic seat was just narrow enough to gouge Dale's hips, and the metal arm supporting the chair groaned every time Dale shifted his weight.

Dale tried to ignore the droning keynote and the unsettled audience, pulling his concentration and awareness into the more constrained world of a laptop screen. People were hard. People were unpredictable. People exhausted him. But white text on a black background?

Controlled.

Soothing.

Dale brought up the file with the source code changes Surge had examined. The code looked tidy and clean to him, as precise and clear as the last Open Group specification for Pluggable Authentication Modules.

But he'd spent months with that code, developing a deep understanding of its quirks. He'd seen that code work flawlessly, and spent days delving into the obscure, hard-to-trigger cases when something went wrong on his network.

Someone coming to this code for the first time would be just as lost as Dale had been.

Dale's proposed changes added several hundred lines of instructions. The hypothetical newcomer would have to do all the work Dale had done, plus more to understand Dale's work.

At the beginning of his addition, Dale added a marker to indicate that the text that followed wasn't meant for the machine, but for human eyes. He added a second marker right after it, to tell the computer it could look again. He then backed up between the markers and typed *High loss physical media require special handling. Implement Forward Implicit Congestion Notification per the specification.* There, that should do it...

No, it shouldn't. If he didn't want people to look more closely, if he didn't want the code dissected, he needed to help people understand what it did. Each extra set of eyes scrutinizing the code was another chance someone might notice a couple of minor oddities he'd left in.

The comments needed to be throughout the section. "Here's what this section does. Here's what this other section does." Lay it out specifically. Tell other programmers almost everything, so that nobody would need to spend much brain power on it.

The secret was already in public view. Make it clear that nobody needed to look for it.

Dale spent the next half-hour in a comforting haze of carefully arranged text, describing and discussing the obvious function of his changes while making sure that all the tidy indentation and formatting remained intact *and* verifying that the machine instructions worked as they had before he started adding his comments. He saved his work, sent it over to a lab machine back in his Detroit office, and launched the test suite.

Performance numbers flickered and danced across his screen.

The code improved performance, yes.

But if someone used it to support a ShufflSoft-based web site, and Dale bumped the web site just right...

A sudden rush of applause shattered his concentration.

Dale jerked up. Where was he? Who were these people? Why did his butt hurt like he'd been sitting on a milk crate?

He shook his head to fling the flash of confusion away.

He'd focused on the terminal and lost the real world. Again.

Stupid ADD.

Droopy-mustached Matheson stood at the bottom of the lecture hall, hands on the podium. The giant projection screen behind him gleamed pale blue, with the word QUESTIONS? across it in four-hundred-point type. His feeble smile showed he hadn't forgotten his worries, but they'd receded for a moment.

The applause faded. Matheson leaned forward, putting his weight on his spindly arms. "One last thing before I give the mic back to Ian." His eyes flickered around the room. "BSD has been around since I was in high school. Yes, I'm known for it today—but that's because the folks who started it moved on. Life does that. But I look around this room, and I see the code I hacked on back in the early nineties all around me. I see people building on what we did. Some of the current BSD projects started twenty years ago, and are still led by the same people. Some have changed leadership teams more than once." His voice grew somber. "What happened this morning with Warren, it shook us all up. Nobody likes being reminded about mortality—don't mistake me, I'm sure he'll be fine, but still." He took a deep breath. "We have our disagreements, but I want you to remember… Remember, we're a community. There's arguments, but we have far more in common than we don't."

Matheson stood straight. "For the next two days, I want everyone to remember: you might never get a chance to speak with each other again. Treat each other well."

The applause was even fiercer than for the open bar announcement.

Dale's chest tightened as he joined it. He had never really felt like he was part of any community.

But he'd shown up here… and they'd welcomed him.

Yes, they'd welcomed his work, but he'd hardly signed in at the registration desk before Mallard and Peterson had called him over and asked his thoughts. Surge had taken time to go through his work, actively considering each bit of it.

Dale had figured out a new way to take control of computers, arranging multiple programs and features in just the right way. It's not that he would use that for any advantage.

But this bunch of operating system professionals, who spent their days suspiciously monitoring systems… they'd welcomed Dale.

Slipping his changes in felt like… a betrayal.

It's no such thing! It's not like I'm going to sell a secret backdoor to the highest bidder. It's just… it's another way for me to get away. It's no different than the key that lets me in any door in the residence hall. It's only if I need to get away, that's all.

Still, SkyBSD ran on, what, one out of ten systems on the public Internet? A tenth of those ran ShufflSoft as well.

Unlimited access to one percent of the Internet was cool. Nobody'd pulled off anything nearly that scale since Ken Thompson's compiler hack, way back when—and Thompson had written the operating system!

Too bad Dale would never be able to tell anyone.

Matheson shuffled back towards his seat.

At any user group Dale had ever attended, someone else always stepped up to take charge when the speaker finished. Today, though, the podium stood empty.

Dale shifted uneasily. Were they supposed to go on to the next talk now? No, nobody else was moving. Other people were peering around the room, like they were wondering as well.

Dale left the test suite running, but disconnected from his home lab. If the time slot for his talk was cancelled, what came next? A quick check of the BSD North web site said lunch started in fifteen minutes.

The guy with the ridiculously long beard next to Dale grumbled under his breath. Dale glanced over, suddenly feeling exposed as the man met his gaze but said nothing.

Dale made himself breathe. "Uh, what's happening now?"

The man's beard flopped with his shrug. "Langton usually comes out to say—oh, there he is!"

Langton let the door drift shut behind him. The gut-punched expression on his face as he trudged to the podium turned Dale's blood cold.

Hands on the podium for support, Langton heaved out a deep breath. He closed his eyes, only opening them after a few seconds.

Dread stopped Dale's breath.

Langton leaned in towards the mic. "I'm sorry to say—very sorry to say…" The sound of his inhalation came clearly through the overhead. "Upon arrival at the hospital this morning, Warren Lash was pronounced dead."

22

Lunch was both spectacular and demoralized.

The folding buffet tables once again lined the side of the MacDonald Hall antechamber. Aromatic steam rose from Sterno-heated stainless steel pans. Round trays supported pyramids of thick sandwiches in wraps and pretzel buns and onion rolls. A little round table to the side bore a *Vegetarian Meals* placard and four small cardboard boxes. Coolers at the end of the table overflowed with ice-covered soda cans.

A couple of attendees had picked up sturdy paper plates from one end of the buffet and picked their way along. Most of the crowd stood in small circles, freshly stunned.

Apparently *Lash is dead, let's eat!* wasn't an effective way to announce lunchtime.

The meager breakfast hadn't satisfied Dale, and his stomach grumbled at the garlic and oregano drifting from the buffet. He should grab something before the crowd shook off their shock, but the thought of eating made him slightly queasy. Even the folks who were at the buffet didn't seem eager, picking only one or two items before wandering off. A group of computer nerds should attack a lunch buffet like they hadn't eaten in weeks, but the folks picking at the food looked… embarrassed?

They *should* be embarrassed.

No, life went on. Someone who hadn't gotten breakfast needed lunch. Dale told himself he shouldn't judge.

The lunchtime crowd had a distinct current, though. While many folks stood in little knots, a fair number of loners wandered up the stairs to the second floor. Dale glimpsed little crowds all the way around, almost all of them standing with their back to the railing.

Was something going on up there?

Dale's stomach twitched again, but he didn't feel like listening to it. Besides, skipping lunch wasn't a bad idea after last night's Festival of Carbs. He wouldn't drop any weight if he kept eating fried potatoes with a side of fried.

Instead, he slipped between quietly talking clusters to slip up the stairs.

More folding tables ran along the outer wall of the second floor mezzanine, each draped in black. Some were flanked by colorful freestanding banners, or had professionally printed signs taped to the stone-clad wall behind them. Some tables had a suspiciously high percentage of suited men beside them. But each table was covered in colorful flyers or computer systems.

He'd found the vendor area.

Vendor salespeople gave Dale a whole different menu of conference frustrations. The glad-handers made his skin try to crawl away and rarely had anything interesting. The smiling meet-your-eye-but-don't-speak should have been better, but more often than not just saying *hello* opened a torrent of words meant to prevent Dale's escape. Vendors Dale actually wanted to talk to, with interesting products, were usually sullen and refused to meet anyone's eyes until you walked up and demanded attention. *Don't talk to me, I'm an engineer, just give me your money for the cool thing I've done.*

Dale knew just how they felt.

To the left of the stairs, a banner over a table proclaimed *192 Cores and Counting!* for the CoreBSD Foundation's fundraising table. Short-haired men in black T-shirts emblazoned with wireframe daemons stood behind and around the table, talking quietly with each other. Dale recognized Max Reinholt, still wearing his sport coat over his T-shirt, talking merrily with a tall chubby man with a babylike face.

On the other side, the SkyBSD Foundation's table drape announced *We Own The Cloud.* A clique of men and women around that table all wore matching green button-down shirts with the SkyBSD daemon stitched over the pocket. Dale had heard that SkyBSD had a bunch of big Internet companies as sponsors, and apparently the foundation members felt they had to look the part. They'd lost any corporate smiles, though.

Stopping for a breath between the tables, Dale caught baffling scraps of conversation.

"—early Senate election—"

"—shame—"

"—didn't like him, but—"

"—bar tonight—"

"—other auction charity—"

Dale turned right, skirting around the SkyBSD table, and meandered down the mezzanine to check out the vendors. If he hugged the railing maybe he could stay out of glad-hander range, or at least quickly escape their gravity well.

The next vendor offered a bunch of cheaply printed computer books in haphazard piles on the bare table. Yet another middle-aged overweight guy, gray hair buzzed short in a sad effort to make his bald patch less obvious, stood behind the table, arms waving as he babbled at a couple of twentysomethings. The guy had been doing the same thing downstairs, to a different group of captives. Even Dale knew that the shuffling feet and averted glances meant they really wanted to escape, but they didn't quite know how.

Better you than me, kid.

No, they're only ten years younger than me. Not kids.

The drape on the next table said *Dakota Internet*, and bore a blanket of cheap pens and little cardboard boxes along with stacks of ad cards. The tiny Latin guy sitting behind the desk looked straight at Dale. "Hey—would you like a flashlight?"

Dale assembled a smile. Yes, he'd have to listen to the spiel, but a flashlight was better than the usual cheap pen. "Sure."

"Here you go. Name's Ron."

"Dale." The flashlight was about the size of his thumb, with a cluster of LEDs choking one end. "Thanks."

"I'm supposed to ask everyone," Ron said. "Do you need hosting?"

"I'm chief engineer at a Detroit Network Services," Dale said automatically. No, that was rude—he should have softened it a little.

"You're doing the abandoned building networking talk," Ron said. "I need to see that."

"The Dakotas have that many abandoned buildings?" Dale said.

"Not like you do. But power independence would be good."

Dale nodded. "I'm kind of fond of it."

"Haven't seen you here before."

At least he hasn't tried to sell me anything. "First time."

Ron grimaced. "Hell of a way to start."

Dale made himself take a deep breath. *Don't go around saying Lash was murdered.* "These things happen."

"Not here they don't. Hey, since you're in the biz, but not in my area—you want a T-shirt?"

"Sure," Dale said. An extra shirt would help.

"Four-X?"

"Three." *Do I look that big?*

Ron bent beneath the table, muffling his voice. "Are you going to talk routers?"

Maybe he was trying to give me a chance to say I'm smaller than four-X? "On site? Yep."

Ron offered Dale a folded bundle. "Three-X. If you don't mind my asking, what kind of border routers are you using?"

The shirt felt very soft. Dakota Internet could afford to pay for the better cloth. "Thanks. It's a mix, Cisco and RouterOS and CoreBSD with their BGPD. What about you?"

"We're SkyBSD with Quagga. Pretty standard colo stuff. Why all the different types?"

Dale shrugged. "We were all Crisco when I started. A week in, someone hit us with a DDOS that took the whole border down. No matter what hits us today, at least one border router stays up."

Ron nodded thoughtfully. "Good idea. We just throw bigger hardware at attacks."

"Yeah, been there," Dale said. "Where do you get your bandwidth?"

Dale forgot himself as the conversation sank into the details of running the Internet and the language became more specialized: bits and packets per second, peering points and transit, cross-country Ethernet and nearest exit routing. Ron paused now and then to greet others and hand out toys, but only for a few seconds before returning to the tech talk.

"Hey." The skinny bald guy, one of the people who had called Dale over for dinner the night before to quiz him about Git, appeared at Dale's elbow. "How you doing, Ron?"

It was—it was… Dale's relaxation evaporated. *You had a long talk with this man last night, dude. How can you have forgotten his name already?* A better question would be, how could he remember names better? The guy had a BSD North badge hanging around his neck. If he turned to face Dale, just a little, he could read the name there. If the badge was turned around the right way.

Ron rescued Dale by saying "Hi, Gerry."

That was it! Gerry… Pterodon? No—Peterson, that was it. Maybe. Dale tried to focus on Gerry's face without nakedly staring, chanting the name to fix it in his memory. "How's it going?"

"Better than some," Peterson said. "You hear about Lash?"

"I was in the back of the room," Ron said. "Terrible thing."

"Yeah," Peterson said. "No idea how this is going to change things."

"What's going to change?" Dale said.

Peterson turned a little more to Dale. "Warren was part of the SkyBSD Senate." His lips tightened. "He was point on the harassment policy mess."

Ron grimaced. "Don't know who else is going to want that."

"That's why they're the Senate," Peterson said. "They get to do what nobody else wants to do."

"Maybe they need to delegate it," Ron said.

Dale shifted his feet nervously. The conversation had moved on. Should he do the same? No, just walking off would be rude. Be patient for a minute. No, don't take a deep breath, that'll sound like a sigh. Just… pay attention for a minute.

Peterson shrugged. "There's enough people pissed off on one side or the other. We might as well get T-shirts that say Team LaCroix or Team Hellman."

Hellman.... where had Dale heard that name?

"It's not urgent," Ron said. "They've both turned in their commit bits. Everyone understands when your point man drops dead."

Hellman... Dale almost jumped with the recollection. "Hellman? You mean Jason Hellman?" *The guy who took me up to the chemical closet when I was freaking out?*

Peterson nodded. "Spoken like someone who has the luxury of not paying attention to this shit."

"He seems like such a nice guy," Dale said. "What happened?"

"Dora and Jason, they got into it on IRC," Ron said. "Jason didn't like how she acted towards some of his friends, she stood up for herself, it went ugly."

"In all fairness," Peterson said, "his so-called friends were posting all sorts of shit about her online."

"No reason to get bitchy about it," Ron said.

"They stole nude pics from her ex's PC," Peterson said. "That's worth getting 'bitchy' about. It all happened because she's a woman."

Dale's face flushed as warring instincts rose.

He hadn't meant to start an argument. How could he end it? Divert it? Escape, somehow? The urge to slip away made his feet twitch.

The other side of his brain reminded Dale that people had discounted him for his ADD brain. They called it a disorder for a *reason*. It was a defect. Getting thrown away for it made a brutal, sick sense, even though Dale couldn't help having that problem. But being female wasn't a disorder, and even if she could help it she shouldn't have to.

Plus, nobody stole nude pics of a guy to post on the Internet.

He really ought to say so.

Dale fumbled for words. "Sounds like Lash had his work cut out for him." *God, Dale, could you be even weaker?*

"You can say that again," Peterson's jaw had tightened, and he'd pulled his shoulders back almost as if he was ready to throw a punch.

"It's a pain," Ron said. "Hey there, you want a shirt?"

Dale glanced at Peterson. The man shut down Pokotylo's crass joke last night. Just now, he'd made his own opinion clear. Technical arguments were one thing, but how did someone stand up in the messy world of human interactions and say *This is right and this is wrong* without a specification to fall back on?

And Ron started a conversation with the guy he'd offered a shirt to. He'd taken the exit Dale offered, while Peterson looked ready to argue on. Peterson had said his mind, and won.

Jealousy stabbed Dale. How did Peterson manage that?

Peterson's gaze spun towards Dale.

The jealously flared to embarrassment—Dale had been staring.

He'd been caught.

Peterson raised his eyebrows inquisitively.

"I met Hellman this morning," Dale said. "He seemed like a nice guy."

Peterson relaxed enough to shrug. "You never can tell about people."

Realization crashed through Dale.

Surge and Lash had argued in the bar last night.

Surge had complained that Lash wanted to make rules against harassment.

Harassment had become an issue because of Hellman.

And Hellman knew where Byward University stored the cyanide.

Dale gave a slow nod. "You're right. You never can tell."

23

Dale's feet led him to circle the exhibit mezzanine, going clockwise with the flow of attendees, but his brain churned elsewhere.

Hellman hadn't wanted to talk to the cops. He hadn't even wanted Dale to talk to the cops. He'd been really, really nervous.

What did Hercule Poirot say? Means, motive, and opportunity, that was it. Hellman knew about the cyanide, and the door to the chemical store was unlocked. Maybe he'd picked the lock, but failed to close the door after. He'd been a student here, so maybe he had an old friend who let him in. Lash had wanted to boot jerks from SkyBSD. Hellman had turned in his commit bit, the equivalent of resigning… but maybe he'd taken that badly.

Opportunity, though…

Hellman had been sitting at the end of a row, up against the wall, near the back of the lecture hall. Dale had trapped him in his seat. But Hellman could have sat down right before Dale got there. No, his laptop had been plugged in. Call it thirty seconds before Dale.

Where had Lash been? Somewhere in that knot of people at the front of the lecture hall. Would Hellman have had the guts to walk up, sprinkle cyanide on Lash's Danish, and stroll away?

Was cyanide even something you sprinkled? Maybe it was a liquid?

A chemistry major would know how to get cyanide in powder form. And Wikipedia probably listed the lethal dose.

Maybe Dale could get into Hellman's machine and check the browser for Wikipedia cookies. Then get into Wikipedia's web server logs. See if Hellman had looked it up.

Dale stopped to shake his head. No, no, no. He didn't have any way to do any of that, not unless Hellman and the Wikipedia sysadmins were all idiots. And the people attending BSD North were among the most likely to properly encrypt their laptops.

And why would Hellman show Dale the chemical closet if he'd raided the chemical closet?

"Hi there!" someone said.

Dale jerked himself back to reality, only realizing too late he'd been caught by a glad-hander. At least the guy offered him a free T-shirt as he babbled about his company's effort to resurrect the Xenix name on a BSD core. Another shirt would be nice—Dale's shirt had soaked through and dried more than once today, but a swamp steamed at the base of his spine beneath his massive laptop backpack.

He accepted a shirt in trade for listening to two minutes of happy talk, a promo card, and a promise to look at the web site.

Xenix? Who in their right mind would bring Xenix back? Might as well try to breathe life into Ultrix. No, VMS.

Other attendees milled down the vendor tables. A few folks leaned against the railing, looking down over the crowd teeming in the lobby. The low murmur below echoed up here, blending into a haze of indecipherable noise. Even up here, though, quiet groups held somber, private conversations.

Part of Dale wondered what they were talking about. All his life, everywhere he'd gone, he'd wandered up against running conversations. His friends said he should just interject himself into them, but Dale had never seen how to do that without being an intrusive jerk.

Dale could only imagine one topic of conversation today, though.

His thoughts about Lash had their own morbid cast, one he didn't want to share. What was he going to say—hey, did you see Hellman sprinkle cyanide on Lash's Danish today? Because the chemical supply was open, and he probably wasn't happy about Lash wanting people like him kicked out of SkyBSD.

Would the hospital do an autopsy? If they did, would they test Lash's blood for poison? Would they do it before the conference ended tomorrow?

If this was a TV show, some perky-pigtailed Goth girl would have the results back before the first commercial break, proving it wasn't only poisoning, it was a rare sort of poisoning only possible from a rare beetle found only within two miles of Hellman's home.

Wherever that was.

The real world didn't work nearly so quickly.

Dale's musing carried him slowly around the mezzanine, here and there letting a vendor draw him in exchange. The folks offering an inexpensive next-generation Non-Volatile Memory Express storage controllers drew his curiosity, but he found himself accepting that T-shirt and wandering on.

Everything came down to: was Lash murdered?

And if so, what was Dale willing to do about it?

Dale made it back to the front stairwell without deciding anything. The crowd below had started to converge on the buffet. His stomach grumbled. Breakfast had been meager, yes, but who knew what dinner would bring? Probably more fried.

Best if he skipped lunch entirely.

The clock said they had another thirty minutes until the next talk started. Maybe he should go back to his room quick. Drop off his six—no, seven—new T-shirts.

He could ignore his stomach for half an hour.

His stomach disagreed. Noisily.

"Bugs and gravel," Dale muttered. He really should find a grocery store nearby and check for protein shakes.

"There you are, Dale!" an accented voice said.

24

Dale jumped in surprise.

The broad staircase yawned beside him, and his feet wobbled on the tile. He seized the top of the rail with one hand, trying to steady himself.

His feet were several inches from the edge of the stairs. Nothing to worry about.

But his heart still pounded.

I hope nobody saw that.

Dale gulped air and glanced around.

Misha Pokotylo stood about three feet away. He'd swapped yesterday's T-shirt for a corporate polo shirt with the ShufflSoft logo, but his biceps still strained against the cotton. The combination of the crowd noise and Pokotylo's Russian accent made Dale squint with effort to understand Pokotylo's words. "You all right?"

"Of course." Dale made himself stand straighter, feebly willing his embarrassment away. "Why wouldn't I be?"

"Good. You see email on commit access?"

Right. ShufflSoft wanted him to get access to make his own changes to their code. "No. No, I'm sorry. I didn't see it this morning?"

Pokotylo chuckled. "I sent during keynote, sorry. Last night ran… very late."

Dale tried to keep his voice steady. "It won't have made it past my graylisting yet, then."

"No matter." Pokotylo waved a hand. "You have OpenPGP key, yes?"

"Of course."

"Is first step for commit bit. Have committer sign your key."

"I still don't think I'm a good candidate." I'm a terrible candidate. I don't want a commit bit, I don't want people to see my name.

"You are committer anywhere else?"

"No."

"You are nervous, that is all," Pokotylo said. "Open benches downstairs. You show me your key and ID, I sign. You have passport?"

"Sure," Dale said. *Just tell him no. How hard is it to just say no?*

"This is only part that needs people together," Pokotylo said. "All else, online. You do the IRC?"

Tell him no. No, nobody's going to believe that. "I'm usually dsw. Like the shoe place—no, you don't have those in Russia, do you?"

"Ukraine!" Pokotylo said. "Not Russia! Soon, we have Western shoe stores. Soon, all the women, they buy stripper heels." His smile got a little brighter.

Great. The guy can't sign a PGP key without getting sleaze on it.

The ShufflSoft mailing list was professional. It had an occasional joke, but mostly the developers discussed technical issues. Dale couldn't help wondering how many of the other developers were just as gross as Pokotylo.

Dale tried to relax his shoulders. He wanted his ShufflSoft patches accepted into the software. It seemed the only way to do that was to take the damned commit bit.

He never had to deal with Pokotylo in person again. It's not like he was doing another tech conference like this.

"Fine."

Dale followed Pokotylo down the stairs, through the painful thought-smothering noise of dozens of voices, and into the corridor where he'd discussed patches with Surge, where he'd first talked with Hellman. The concrete-walled corridor with its slat wooden benches was becoming annoyingly familiar. He might as well hang up a placard and declare it his office. Bring in a plant to help cover up the distant reek of floor wax.

But at least it was a little quieter.

Pokotylo sprawled on one end of a bench, just past a couple of guys gnawing relentlessly on sandwiches, and slipped his thin ultralight notebook out of his pricey leather shoulder bag. "Right. You have key ID?"

Dale heaved his backpack down on the far end of the bench. A blast of cool air shocked his sweaty back. "Sure, let me look that up—no, wait." He unzipped an outer pouch of the bag. A handful of USB flash drives tumbled out. "Crap. Not that." Face hot, he bent to pluck the keys off the floor and stuff them back in the pocket. Where had he put them? Right—this bag had a special pocket inside the third compartment.

Seconds later, he triumphantly pulled out a bent business card. "Here you go."

"You still have business cards?" Pokotylo said.

"For sales meetings. My PGP fingerprint is on the back."

"Ah! Is good idea." Pokotylo accepted the card and brushed his fingers across the tiny laptop's chiclet keyboard. "Yes. Let me get key. Passport?"

"Right." Dale fumbled in the side pocket of his cargo pants. Yes, he hadn't lost it yet. The passport's plastic cover had its own dampness—had he been sweating that much? Pokotylo seemed intent on his laptop, so Dale tried to surreptitiously swipe the passport across his pants.

"Here we are!" Pokotylo said. "Dale S Whitehead, on the MIT keyserver?"

"Among others," Dale said. "Here you go."

Pokotylo studied Dale's passport and frowned. "Here it says middle name is Shirley."

Dale grimaced. "I don't use the middle name."

"Why not?"

Was he serious? Pokotylo was Ukrainian, he had no idea. "Shirley is a woman's name."

Pokotylo's eyebrows drew together in puzzlement. "Your parents give you woman's name?"

"It's also a last name," Dale said. "My mom's maiden name."

"Like the John Shirley." Pokotylo shook his head and offered Dale the passport back. "I can't sign this. You get key with name that matches your real name, I sign."

Dale standing here wasn't good enough to prove he was himself? "Other people have signed it," Dale said.

Pokotylo shook his head again. "People you know? You have never been committer, so I explain." His voice took on a patronizing tone. "We use PGP to conclusively identify people. Is not good tool, but is only tool we have. When you get passport, you use middle name, nyet? Is same thing."

Dale grimaced. "Fine." Nobody looked at PGP keys anyway. "I'll add that as an alias to my current key, okay?"

"Is fine."

"Just a minute." Dale sat, keeping a good arm's reach from Pokotylo, fuming. Yes, according to the specification, Pokotylo was correct. But it's not like anyone really used PGP these days. Dale wasn't doing relief work in the Congo or anything like that, he was just writing software. With quick keystrokes he woke the laptop and brought up the PGP program. *Now how did you add an alias?*

"Is the dash dash edit dash key flag," Pokotylo said.

Dale's annoyance flared brighter. "I'm getting there."

"Just helping."

Dale made himself silent. Yes, Pokotylo had been right. Annoyance made him screw up typing the four-sentence passphrase, so he had to try it a second time. He did it correctly on the third try, though, and was able to add the full legal name from his passport and upload it to the server. "Grab it now."

Pokotylo was already typing. "Got it. Here." He offered Dale an orange passport with a thin strip of paper sticking out of the top. "You sign mine, yes?"

Etiquette said that if someone signed your key, you signed theirs. "Sure." Now what was *that* command?

He took vicious but private pleasure in scrutinizing Pokotylo's passport and comparing it to the name on the digital key. Sadly, they matched perfectly, both the English and the cryptic Cyrillic versions.

He'd almost finished when Pokotylo said, "All set! You check email for committer info. If you like I can give help with first commit. You know the Git?"

Dale had used a few Git functions to create patches, but had never actually done the other side, accepting those patches into a project. But the longer he spent with Pokotylo, the more likely the guy was to say something else offensive. "No, I think I'm good."

"Shufflsoft on EFNet," Pokotylo said cheerfully. "You have trouble with first few, we help, no?"

"Sure." Dale had many people who could swear at Git with him. Lots of people used it, how hard could it be?

"I talk next," Pokotylo said. "I give talk on ShufflSoft hooks for SkyBSD RAIDZed4. You go?"

"I haven't decided yet," Dale said. "Haven't even looked at the schedule."

Pokotylo shrugged. "You go to another talk, I see you later anyway."

Not if I see you first. "Sure."

Pokotylo slid his tiny laptop into his bag and sauntered back towards the main hall. Dale spent a few moments packing up his oversized model into his backpack before pulling out his tablet to check the schedule. The routing daemon talk—yes, he'd wanted to see that. Room 103, in about three minutes.

Dale glanced up. The room across the hall was numbered 191. The talks must be down the other hall.

The crowd in the main room rapidly drained into the main lecture hall and down the other side corridor. A pyramid of drained soda cans balanced atop the recycle bin near the door. Flimsy cardboard plates overflowed the trash bin. A cluster of university caterers lurked near the main door, ready to dive in and suck the remnants of the buffet away once the next talks began.

Dale's stomach let out a tremendous grumble at the sight of the half-eaten lunch buffet. He wavered. After that minimal breakfast, if he skipped lunch, he'd probably find himself feeding those weird Canadian dollar coins into a vending machine for whatever unhealthy snacks were left.

Maybe eating half a sandwich now was a better idea.

25

If the main auditorium had been designed to be impressive, room 103 looked engineered for stark efficiency. The dingy drop ceiling with fluorescent panels made the furniture extra dismal and sucked the colors from people's faces. The ranks of laminate tabletops and attached swing-out plastic seats lacked only oars and shackles to achieve complete academic drudgery.

The room even smelled of boredom.

At an empty seat in the back, Dale carefully lowered the heaped plate of sandwiches onto the tabletop. It's not like egg salad on sliced wheat was a real sandwich, not like the pastrami on onion roll and roast beef and stuff that everyone else had eaten. Four skinny little sandwich halves barely counted. And he'd taken an apple rather than a few of the itty-bitty brownies, or the cookies, or those decadent-looking layered fruity baked things.

Somehow, culinary virtue felt simultaneously unsatisfying and degrading. Like he'd failed. If he'd gorged on brownies, at least his blasted stomach would stop complaining.

Too late now. The caterers were already moving in on the wreckage.

Sugar would have perked up his flagging energy, though.

Probably best he hadn't thought of that rationalization while looking at the brownies.

Dale had barely got his laptop plugged into the power strip when a skinny guy whose glasses barely broke up the cascade of facial hair stood up at the front and said "Hi, everyone. This is the talk on the OmniBSD routing daemon. If you want a different talk, leave now." He stood silent for a moment, glancing around the room.

Dale shook his head. Geek humor. Best known for not being funny.

The guy tapped his clicker, bringing a slide onto the projector. "I'm Donny Eisenfeldt, and I mostly work on embedded systems. If something works on one of my itty-bitty ARM boards, it'll work anywhere."

Dale had told Will he'd check his email a few times during the day, in case any critical problems arose. Dale could do that while listening to the presentation.

The techs seemed on top of everything important, and Will would handle the customer complaining that she was only getting thirty-one megabits from her twenty megabit connection. He considered dropping Will a note, but what was he going to say? *Good talks. Someone dropped dead in the opening ceremony.*

No.

Instead, he logged into his office lab.

The test system had survived running with his newly-commented patches. Comments shouldn't change how code performed, but in reality innocuous changes broke software all too frequently. These had worked, so he should submit them.

Dale brought up his IRC client, a black screen with white text. Where had Surge said? Oh yeah: BSDNorth, one word. Joining the channel made words appear at the bottom of his screen.

#BSDNorth

49 members

Topic: vote Warren Lash Memorial Fund

ham11> Any food left?

Apparently user ham11 was also hungry.

Seconds later, everything scrolled up as someone added another line of comment to the bottom.

jackon> Anyone seen Ian?

Disjointed conversations began flowing past as people threw their own contributions into the channel: asking and answering questions, commenting on ongoing talks, or just trash-talking each other. Typical free range nerdery.

BigSpatula> ospf on a rpi? is this guy insane? link state table overflow wtf

Dale looked up guiltily. The presenter's reedy voice wobbled up and down as he used a green laser pointer to underline parts of a complicated memory diagram on the screen. Yeah, OSPF on a Raspberry Pi? How could you cram something that big into that little memory? It'd have to be a small network. One tiny enough to not need OSPF in the first place.

Keeping his eyes on the presenter, he typed *Is Surge around?*

Listening to the presenter, Dale felt unwillingly impressed. The man had done some really clever things to compress a small routing table into incredibly limited hardware. Not necessarily good things, or stable, or anything Dale would want to run in production or anywhere near his network—but clever.

A moment later he glanced down to read through the IRC buffer. Right in the middle of a half-screen ASCII image of guy's wiener that FlamingSkul had pasted into the channel appeared the text:

surge> Yep.

Dale typed _surge_ *Dale. I have the commented patches. You want them in email or on the bug?*

His message appeared in the chat with the letters dsw> before it.

The presenter said, "Now, we had some problems using this in production."

Dale looked back up. Failures were always interesting. Someone else's failures were the best failures.

The presenter said, "One of our techs put a switch with a leaf configuration on an ancillary network right next to the core. We shared the same auth string in all the areas, so the OSPF on that network—"

Dale had made that mistake nine years ago, and one of the baby techs had done the same four months ago. Yeah, that would eat a bunch of Pis alive, and probably even bring down the whole network. He glanced back at the IRC. Between two people flinging crude insults at each other he found:

surge> Great! on the bug report. always on the bug report. tell me when and I'll look

The presenter was still going through his perfectly expectable OSPF failure. Dale switched to a web browser and attached the file containing his commented patch to his previous submission.

ham11> dOOOOONGs

dsw> _surge_: added

nmbclust> ham11: tuna can

deck> ATTENTION: CoreBSD pub crawl leaves 10PM sharp, straight from dinner

Dale typed his thanks and leaned back in the chair.

The presenter said, "Now, I wouldn't run Pis for routing in production. But that same code worked just fine on some little Soekris boxes."

Routing on a Soekris? Dale sat up straight, peering between the people in the next row. A couple of Dale's remote interconnects could really use a low-power route reflector. A Soekris would do nicely.

He fumbled at his plate, but the sandwiches had gone somewhere. Had someone taken his lunch? No, Dale tasted egg on his tongue.

He'd eaten without realizing it. Again.

Attention deficit disorder several million, Dale zero. But at least today's mayhem hadn't scrambled his ability to understand people.

Grimacing, he snatched the apple and chomped.

"We can hold three full BGP tables on a 3697," the presenter said, green laser wobbling over the columns of text on the slide. "That's IPv4 and IPv6, although to be fair, the IPv6 table still isn't very…"

Three BGP tables? That would do. Dale would have to download the latest OmniBSD and see if it solved his problems. Fixing the messed-up interconnect on top of the Redford Theater alone would pay for his trip here.

His eyes wandered back down to the IRC screen. He'd missed another ASCII wiener and a discussion about virtual memory backpressure algorithms. Now a couple people were debating the virtues of Soekris hardware versus the new BeagleBones. Probably a couple of the guys right here in this room.

Dale scrolled back up to catch the earlier parts of the virtual memory discussion—good information, once you dug between the wieners and smack talk. The noise had bothered him when he first found IRC, but he'd learned to let it wash off him.

Dale frowned.

People in this channel were fairly well-behaved today. At its worst, IRC got really gross. Some people really enjoyed racing to the bottom. And arguments in IRC got vicious and personal—more vicious and personal than in real life, because in IRC nobody could punch you in the face.

Dale could easily imagine two people having a knock-out drag-out argument through the screen, and that argument getting really vile really quickly.

That kind of argument would easily carry over into other social media.

If two developers tightly tied to one project really got into it, the project leadership would have to get themselves involved.

And anyone who really dug into the matter would come smack up against the festering open sewer of IRC. The easiest way to find someone who had that in-depth understanding of some of the more complex topics was to ask online.

You'd get an answer. And you'd get giant ASCII wieners.

Dale set the stripped apple core down thoughtfully and wiped his fingers on the napkin.

Lash had been working on a harassment policy. ASCII wieners might be meant as funny, but nobody really wanted to look at them. Had Lash taken a good look at IRC, at the project culture, and decided to do something about it?

26

The routing talk ended in about half an hour, even with the few questions. Dale had a whole hour until the next talk. A few of the attendees had gone up to the podium to ask the presenter some questions, even though he'd closed the talk because the audience had run out of questions. As usual. Dale felt too worry-worn to join in.

He could hang out in the empty presentation room until the next talk. It had all the charm of a prison chapel, but that was university for you. But which talk *was* next? Tugging the tablet from his pocket, he scrolled down to the next time slot.

Next up in Room 103: abusing sed and awk.

Not a chance. Dale routinely abused sed and awk. He'd probably slip into a coma halfway through that session, unless the Torquemada chair kept him alert.

But if he sat here for a while, the next presenter would show up. Dale would have to pack up and walk away, with the presenter watching him and wondering why one of the audience members had abandoned his talk before it began.

Nobody deserved that.

Even someone presenting on sed and awk.

Room 101 had a talk on debugging Perl next. If Dale had to debug Perl, he was solving the wrong problem. 102, the perennial panel on historical computing hardware. Someone would bring out their 1890 mechanical calculator and act like it was cool. The main lecture hall had a ZedFS introduction. Dale didn't need a ZedFS introduction, he needed a "here's how you vivisect filesystems" session.

The time slot after that? Three talks that looked great, and another talk.

So, the question was: which talk would Dale sit in next, while he waited for an interesting talk? Accidentally hearing part of the sed/awk talk would probably make his blood pressure spike.

Maybe the ZedFS introduction would work. He might even learn something.

Until then? Maybe he'd go through the vendors again. That storage controller had piqued his interest. Try to forget about murder for a while.

Dale slowly packed his laptop, carefully coiling the power cable and fastening it with the Velcro tie. The seven new T-shirts stuffed into the second compartment made zipping the backpack shut almost impossible. He really had to clean out the stuff he didn't use very often.

Sunlight shone through the overhead skylights of the main hall, reflecting off the side wall and the floor to brighten the stone-clad walls. A handful of conference goers wandered aimlessly, studying the plaques of famous Byward University chemistry grads or just stretching their legs. Dale felt disappointed to see the catering crew clearing the last of lunch. It was for the best, he didn't need any more food—but no, there at the end, one table stood with the last of the buffet arranged neatly on it.

You do not need a snack, mister.

But there's a vat of iced drinks on the floor by it. Maybe a cola would give him some oomph.

Fine. But no damn brownies. You're not hungry anyway, and you know it.

The brownies were gone, but the chocolate cookies were so soft that the ones hanging over the edge of the tray bent under their own weight. There were two stacked trays of those round baked parfait things with the crumbly topping. The meat sandwiches had gone, but a pyramid of egg salad ones remained. Which made sense—egg salad didn't satisfy anyone.

Dale gritted his teeth and plunged his hand into the icy cold of the drinks cooler. Fruit juice, hi-calorie thirst quencher—no. He sorted between full-sugar sodas until he found one lone diet.

You have your drink. Now walk away.

Surely one brownie wouldn't—

No. No, no, no. The group dinner tonight was probably fried lard, with a side of fried.

Walk. Away.

He'd barely taken a second step when a voice behind him said, "Dale?"

Ian Langton was walking up quickly from the far side of the buffet, a big guy trailing right behind him. "You're Dale Whitehead, right?"

"Yeah?"

Langton stopped right next to the dessert display. "Dale, this is Rob Deck."

The man was taller than Dale, with short-cropped blond hair and a meticulously groomed goatee. An Arrogant Worms T-shirt hung over his belt to conceal a potbelly, but he still seemed full of energy and strength. "Howdy."

"Hi."

"I have to ask a favor," Langton said.

What could Dale do? "Sure."

Langton lowered his voice enough that Dale could barely hear. "We need to have someone pack up Warren's things."

Dale flinched. Did they want him to do that? He took half a step closer to hear better. The heady smells of baked sugar and chocolate assaulted his nose.

He breathed deeply to steady himself, but that only made the problem worse.

Langton said, "Housekeeping can do that. But that leaves us with two half-empty suites. I'd like to move you in with Deck for tonight. Give you a different room, and save a few bucks for next year."

But I have my own shower now! Dale bit back the words before they escaped. Would he really sleep better in a suite with a murdered man's vacant bed? And Langton's request was annoyingly reasonable.

Deck said, "I really don't mind." Had he misunderstood Dale's hesitation?

Dale straightened. "Sure."

Langton smiled. "Great! We appreciate it."

The sugary aroma was making Dale dizzy. "Not a problem."

"I've got the room right next to the bath," Deck said. "The other door's shut, but just walk right in, it's all yours, eh?"

"Okay." Maybe one cookie?

"The hard part," Langton said, "is that most of the housekeeping staff goes home at five." His voice dropped to just above a whisper. "I'd like to get Warren's stuff over to the, the morgue tonight, so it can all go home with him. And I'd hate for housekeeping to get some of your belongings by mistake."

Lash's family had enough grief. They didn't need one of Dale's sweat-stinking shirts mysteriously added to it. "The next few talks aren't that interesting. Why don't I go now?"

"Thank you," Langton said. "Get the key at the front desk, move your stuff, turn your old key in."

He'd have to fix the new key. "Sure."

"Room 1309," Deck said.

"I'm on it." Dale nodded, turning from the buffet in dissatisfied victory.

27

Ottawa's warm June sun and the brisk breeze infused Dale with a hit of vitality, and the diet soda's aluminum aftertaste promised caffeine's warm rush. Behind the residence hall reception desk, a tiny Asian woman offered Dale a friendly smile, which turned somber when he offered his name. "I'm sorry," she said as she gave him the new key. "Once you've moved, bring me the old key. We'll take care of everything."

Dale pondered as the elevator rose to the fourteenth floor. His old room first. Pack up his stuff. Then the new room. Get the new T-shirts out of his backpack, leave them—no, put one on. After this morning, he deserved a clean shirt.

If Lash had been murdered, the killer was almost certainly back at the conference. The residence hall was probably the safest place in the world right now.

The fourteenth floor felt different from this morning. The only sound was the muffled hum of the air conditioner grouchily shuffling stale air tinted with industrial cleaner. The hallway's thin carpet swallowed the sound of Dale's footsteps. He'd never been in a mausoleum, but he imagined that a tomb would feel much like this.

You're being silly. Stop it.

Room 1408. Lash's last stop.

Unwilling to disturb the silence, Dale slipped his card through the scanner and gently eased the heavy door open.

He'd taken two steps in before he realized that the new sounds didn't belong.

The quick chime of a booting Apple.

Someone grunted.

Something thudded.

Dale froze, his feet on the white tile of the common room.

The door to Lash's room was pushed almost closed.

It had been wide open when they'd left this morning.

The door muffled indistinct words, but Dale felt pretty sure the last one was an annoyed "Boot!"

Dale's breath stopped, but his heart jackrabbited in his throat and his every muscle trembled.

Lash had said on the way to the conference that he had a second computer. Surely there was a legitimate reason for someone to be in his room, after his death, trying to get into that machine.

But Dale's gut screamed: *killer*.

The empty hallway suddenly felt cavernous, the yards between him and the elevator like miles. Other than Dale and the intruder, the floor was abandoned.

Dale made himself hold still and think. If there was a valid reason for someone to be in his room, the front desk would know.

If the person was an intruder, the front desk could call the police.

Dale could back out. Call the front desk.

Then, if he felt brave: stand at the end of the hall. Poke at his phone. Wait. Watch.

His heart beat even faster.

If security didn't arrive in time, Dale could get a look at the intruder.

He just had to lurk at the end of the hall. Like he belonged there. Like he was waiting for someone. Look up hopefully when the door to 1408 opened, then disappointed.

Maybe mutter *Dammit Fred, where are you?*

Remember the intruder's face.

If he was really lucky, or unlucky, it might be someone Dale knew.

If Dale kept his cool, he might even be a hero.

The voice said "Okay, which one?"

A man's voice? Probably. The door mostly muffled it.

Dale tried to swallow, but his mouth was so dry it ached. Paying careful attention to his feet, trying to move silently, he took two quick steps back into the hall.

His shoes touched carpet before he realized his mistake.

The heavy door was gliding shut.

Dale flung a hand out to catch it.

He still had the stupid key card in his fingers.

Just as the flimsy card touched wood, the door thudded into the frame.

The sound echoed through the hall.

Please, please—

An almost-muffled call from inside 1408.

Dale fled.

Maybe the intruder wouldn't—

But as Dale turned the corner, a door clicked open behind him.

28

Dale ran down the barren hall.

Elevator? No, he'd have to wait for it to arrive and the intruder was right behind him, just around the corner, seconds away and there was the stairwell, but he'd never make it down before someone caught him so he ran right past.

Had the intruder glimpsed him going around the corner?

Maybe he was going the other way around the loop. If Dale kept running, he might faceplant straight into the guy.

No, Dale couldn't keep running. His heart fluttered, and fuzzy grayness seemed to fill his temples—breathe. He had to breathe.

Poison was a coward's weapon.

But cornered cowards get mean.

Instinctively, Dale swerved to the next room. His head whirled, but his hand slipped the key card right through the lock.

Maybe his database hacks hadn't been good enough.

Maybe someone had found his change to the registration system. Undone it.

The tiny LED by the slot flickered.

Green.

Dale slammed his shoulder into the door and charged into someone else's room.

On his first step he pivoted, crashing his backpack against the doorframe and staggering, keeping his feet thanks to some primal wiring in the bottom of his brain—*thank you grandpa monkey*—shoving the door shut and letting it thud into place.

Dale's head still swam. His throat and chest burned as if he floated in vacuum, his gut knotted so tight he stooped a little, arms crossed protectively across his chest as he strained to hear over his own thunderous pulse.

Breathe. He had to breathe or he'd pass out.

Dale forced his chest to open—slowly, slowly. Don't gasp. Don't make any noise. The suite's air felt hot and weighted.

The killer's outside. In the hall. Maybe right outside.

The door had a peephole.

Dale painfully eased in a breath, then another. The fuzziness in his head receded just enough to clear his vision, but fresh sweat burned into his eyes.

Still no noise outside.

Then someone grunted.

Dale's heart leaped again, but he made himself straighten and lean into the door. He had to blink to focus through the peephole.

Dale glimpsed someone at the edge of the fish-eye view, but they were already walking away.

He pressed his palms against the door, leaning, trying to calm himself and slow his heart before he ruptured something.

Nothing in the hall.

Still nothing.

Dale stood there a moment, until his head cleared and his pulse slowed to mere marathon pace. He really had to get in shape sometime. Somehow.

He kept his attention on the fisheye view of the hall until his eye watered too badly and he had to pull back and squeeze the lids together to recover.

Out in the hall, the elevator dinged.

Dale's heart pattered a moment, but he felt too exhausted to panic again.

But he was in someone else's suite.

The suite was a mirror image of Dale's, with the bathroom to the left instead of the right. No furniture, only industrial white laminate and metal appliances gleaming in the dim daylight diffusing from the bedrooms at the back.

No place to hide. Not even a closet.

Dale swallowed and leaned back to the peephole.

What would he do if someone came to this door? Put their keycard in?

Maybe run for the bathroom. No, someone coming back to their room probably needed a few moments at the throne.

Pick a bedroom. Either bedroom. Fifty-fifty chance. Lurk until the person left, or maybe until they went into the bath and shut the door.

A shadow covered the peephole.

Dale's breath stopped.

The shadow moved on.

Dale tried to deliberately relax. If his body kept knotting up like this, he'd give himself a heart attack or something.

A door thudded shut somewhere.

Dale suddenly felt exposed. He'd never expected to need to get into other rooms, but now that he had his skin kept crawling and the sensation of being watched burned between his shoulder blades.

But what if the intruder was still out there?

Indecision made him wobble on his feet.

Can't go. Can't stay.

The elevator dinged.

No, if he stayed they'd find him stroked out on the floor.

He pressed his eye to the peephole, but nobody came.

After another moment, Dale eased the door open and peeked out.

Empty hallway.

He let the door thud shut behind him. Even the hallway's stale air felt fresh after the confines of the stranger's suite.

Where now?

He still had to move. The front desk was waiting for him to get down with his stuff.

Surely the intruder wouldn't go right back to Dale's suite?

He probably did. But he wouldn't remain.

Dale made himself walk slowly up the hall. Around the corner.

Standing outside his suite, he strained his ears but heard nothing beyond his own rattletrap breath.

Barely daring to breathe, he slipped his card through the lock and eased the door open.

Silence.

The door to Lash's room stood open, sunlight illuminating the built-in desk.

A power cable sat plugged into the wall, the cord disarrayed. A few connectors and cables lay scattered.

But Lash's spare laptop was gone.

29

Dale heaved his backpack onto the desk in his own room and planted his hands beside it, head drooping. His face felt sticky with sweat—not normal sweat, but thick greasy stuff. Was that what they meant by fear-sweat? His shirt, drenched. His heart had slowed, but his whole body ached with the adrenaline's aftermath.

Once, back in Detroit, a rooftop had proven less solid than he'd expected. He'd never forget that sickening feeling of a building shifting beneath him, the whole structure oozing to the side. He'd ran back to a more solid part of the roof and climbed straight down, but afterwards his whole body had felt like he'd run a marathon at gunpoint.

Right now, he felt worse.

Was that blood he tasted? Had he bitten himself? No, his tongue felt swollen and heavy but whole.

Get yourself together, man. Someone was in your room. They're not here now. They stole Lash's spare laptop and left.

Dale spent another minute steadying his breath before standing straight and peeling off his shirt. Shower? No, he hadn't brought enough underwear or socks to change.

The next time he left home, he was bringing a dozen extra sets of clothes.

Not that he was ever leaving home again. Ever.

Dale grabbed a towel to scrape himself dry. A long drink of stale water from the kitchenette sink eased the pounding in his temples. The untidy heap of dirty clothes stalled him for a moment, but he pulled the bag from the unused bedroom trash can and wadded the smelly pile into it. The empty hallway felt menacing, but he brought the ungainly bundle down to 1309 without seeing anyone.

Suite 1309 was arranged just like 1408 and furnished in the same Easy-Clean Ape-Proof Industrial Style, but the afternoon sun had already moved past the windows. What time was sunrise around here, anyway? Deck had claimed the bedroom closest to the bathroom, the one Dale had taken on the floor above, so Dale dragged everything into the other room.

He sagged onto the bed. The spread was just as rough as the one in his other room. The pillows looked just as rocky. His heart had slowed, but his brain still whirled. The ache had spread from his muscles into his joints, his bones. Maybe he needed some aspirin or something.

No, what he needed was to get out of here. Forget getting his patches into SkyBSD and ShufflSoft. Change his flight, or just rent a car. It was only, what, six hundred miles? Ten hour drive, even with Canada's annoying speed limits.

Leave tonight.

Now.

Slow down. Don't go charging off stupidly. Charge off smartly. Can you change your flight? Claim an emergency? If not, who rents cars internationally? Or you can always rent something to Windsor and catch the tunnel bus, then a taxi home.

Dale's hands shook. So did his neck, his head, his shoulders.

The thought that someone had murdered Lash had been unreal all day. Yes, the chemical closet was unlocked, but that could have been coincidence. The drama of a possible murder had absorbed him.

But someone had broken into their suite and taken Lash's laptop.

Chased Dale out of the suite.

Dale had barely escaped without being seen.

This wasn't a hypothetical maybe-murder any more. The uncertainty had made the thought of murder almost... not palatable, but—mere drama? Dale had been able to tell himself to stop being a drama king.

But the drama was very real.

And he wasn't the king of it. Not even close.

BSD North would end tomorrow evening. The attendees that didn't leave right after would evaporate the next morning.

The hospital had Lash's body. Eventually, they'd run an autopsy.

They'd figure out he was killed.

But the suspects would be scattered all over the world.

Acid burned Dale's stomach.

Right now, the only person who knew, absolutely totally *knew*, that Lash had been murdered was Dale.

And the murderer.

Lash hadn't been a bad guy. Yeah, he'd been that annoying kind of friendly, the sort that Dale didn't really know how to deal with— no, really, he didn't know how to deal with most any kind of friendly, but still, Lash hadn't known, hadn't had any way to know, that being friendly made Dale uncomfortable.

Lash had only known Dale was new, and had tried to ease his way into the conference.

He'd taken point on the SkyBSD's project's response to online harassment, and seemed intent on actually doing something about it.

Dale couldn't see that he'd done anything to warrant a death sentence.

And even if he had... didn't he deserve to have his murder solved?

And Lash aside: didn't a murderer deserve to be caught?

Right now, Dale was the only person in the whole world who knew there was a murderer.

In a few days, everyone would know.

And everyone, including Lash's wife and children, would know the murderer had gotten away with it.

And Dale would have to live with that.

Or figure out something to do about it.

30

Full of fresh determination, Dale heaved open MacDonald Hall's heavy front door to have his nose assaulted by sugar.

The conference crowd looked almost as dense as it had been during breakfast, but the day's events had drained animation from people's faces. Conversations had risen above funeral home whispers, but didn't come near the morning's boisterous if sleepy cheer. A skinny guy in jeans and an Adorable Linux T-shirt stood near the entrance with a small paper plate in one hand, using the plastic fork in the other to emphasize his words as he talked to one of the nattily-suited Indian men. Dale caught a few words, something about problems in library versioning. Mister Adorable Linux seemed intent on bludgeoning his opinion into the other man.

Of course shared library symbol versioning caused problems. That's what symbol versioning was *for*. But the problems it created were less pernicious than the problems it solved.

A tall woman, thin to the point of gauntness, strode out of the crowd with her own paper plate and claimed a quiet spot near one of the pillars supporting the mezzanine.

Cake. Someone had generously brought cake for the afternoon break.

Someone was a bastard.

Dale really wasn't hungry. He just… *wanted*.

He tugged his tablet out of his cargo pocket in a deliberate attempt to distract himself. Three talks he might like to see closed out the day's programming: one on resource locking in CoreBSD's experimental 512-processor support, another on improvements to nested virtualization in SkyBSD, and a third on software-based frame switching. Plus a fourth talk, on an experimental port of the SkyBSD source tree to Git, but Dale would rather be left alone with the cake and an alibi than sit through yet another talk on source code management tools—especially with all the people who wanted SkyBSD to switch to Git.

But he could pick a talk, go in early, claim a spot, and get to work.

Killers don't catch themselves.

Dale grimaced. The first three talks sounded interesting, which meant any of them would do. The kernel locking talk was in the big lecture hall, with decent power and wireless. It had a side door, so he could avoid the cake trap. He hunched his shoulders and plunged into the crowd.

"Dale!" someone called.

Dale stopped, glancing around.

Someone bumped into his backpack, making him take a clumsy half step.

Who was it? "Sorry," Dale said over his shoulder.

The guy behind him silently scuttled around Dale.

There—Langton was coming up to him, one hand raised. Dale should have expected that. "How did it go?" Langton said.

Lash's killer was pillaging his victim's room, stole his laptop, and chased me. "Fine."

"You gave them the old key card back?"

"Yep. The girl at the desk, she was calling housekeeping as I came back."

"Good." Langton dropped his voice. "Thanks again for moving."

"Whatever I can do to help." That phrase had always struck Dale as vacuous, a meaningless social lubricant used by people that didn't want to do anything. It suddenly felt weighted, a surprise oath.

Dale had something he could do.

And to his own surprise, he was going to do it.

"You're doing plenty," Langton said. "Did you get your wristband?"

"Wristband?" He'd missed something else?

"You need one to get into dinner tonight. Sharon has them, the table right by the cake. Did you get cake?"

No! No, I didn't, and I deserve a piece. "I—I think I need to pass."

"Be sure you get your wristband, though." Something behind Dale caught Langton's eye. "I need... I need to get on something. Talk to you later."

"Later," Dale said.

Shuffling around the crowd, Dale made out a woman sitting at the buffet table, at the far end from the cake. He slipped up to her and exchanged his name for a bright blue rubbery wristband imprinted with BSD NORTH, somehow escaping without getting tractor-beamed into the cake line, then made his way to the top tier of the lecture hall so he could settle into the last row.

What he needed to do, he didn't want anyone shoulder-surfing. A couple other guys were already camped in the back, heads bent together so they could break into the Federal Reserve or something without anyone noticing, but the far left corner was empty. Perfect.

He just had the laptop running and connected to the conference network when a couple more attendees strode into the lecture hall, laughing loudly. "Seconds on cake are open!" one called. "And they're trying to get rid of it, so they're big slices now."

Dale deliberately concentrated on how the tabletop pressed against his gut. Remember the conference dinner tonight. You don't need cake. Not even a big slice.

"*Ridiculously* big slices."

Dale drew a deep breath and focused. Log into the home machine. Bounce from there to Indonesia, then the Czech Republic, and finally back to that Canadian machine and into the Byward University facilities network.

He'd done this same work only the day before. His fingers flew, and he glided right into the residence hall management system.

Someone had been in his suite.

The only way to open the suite was with a key card.

The management system recorded every key swipe.

All Dale needed to do was identify the key cards that had opened 1408 this afternoon. Whoever had gone in right before Dale was his suspect.

Dale had never examined the tables that stored the key access records, though. By the time he figured out how the system had stored the data, the room was half-full and the presenter paced at the podium, waiting out his final minute of freedom.

No matter. Dale could dig into this and listen to the talk. All he needed was to figure out the right select statement to pull all the accesses of his suite, and join that with checking the key card numbers against the registration database. Technically easy—the hard part was understanding how the database designers had stored all the information. After a few failed attempts, he pulled up neat columns of every key card swipe in his room for the month of June.

He ignored the earliest results—that data was meaningless anyway, he hadn't correlated the card numbers with historical registration data. But at the end…

Yesterday in suite 1408, Dale had swiped in at 16:31:11: check-in. The next swipe was Warren Lash at 16:33:41: testing his card before he hit the bar. Dale had swiped at 17:01:29: testing that his card still worked after he'd modified the privileges. Dale had come back from the Royal Oak at 21:11:01. Lash had swiped in this morning at 01:33:48—no wonder Dale hadn't heard him.

The next two swipes were Dale, this afternoon.

Nobody else had swiped a card this afternoon.

Puzzled, Dale leaned back. The plastic chair groaned beneath him, and he lurched forward, glancing around wildly. The audience seemed intent on the speaker's mellifluous voice and the slide listing umpteen billion ways to lock kernel threads.

Nobody had noticed.

He made his shoulders unclench and rolled his head. Relax. Think.

Someone had gotten into his room. Either they'd played Spider-Man and slipped in the window through a hole too small for Dale's head, or they'd gotten in the door. If no card swipes were recorded in his suite, either someone had a card that didn't record its swipes or they'd tampered with the records.

Dale pondered. Setting up a card whose swipes weren't recorded was the more difficult job. The hacker would have to adjust the software, not just the data. But if they'd tampered with the records, evidence might remain. He wrote another query to grab all of today's card swipes in the residence hall.

Thousands of lines of output flashed down his screen, made bursty by the international detours in his connection. Dale grimaced—stupid, thoughtless, noob error. Even in the summer, people constantly entered the residence halls. And left, but only the entrances required card swipes. His fingers itched to interrupt the query, but that might disrupt the fragile chain of connections.

Fuming, he watched the spew of useless output. When it finished, he repeated the query but sent the output to a file on his laptop.

The next part should be annoying and tedious, but Dale had already written a script to handle a similar task with phone records. He made a new copy of the script, tweaked the analysis format, and ran it.

Inhumanly fast, the laptop spit out its answer.

Each day, the system assigned each key card swipe a unique number. The first card swipe after midnight was request 1, the second request 2, and so on. The system used these numbers as an index.

The records for swipes 8611, 10133, and 11869 were missing.

Someone had tampered with the records.

Despair made Dale sag.

It had seemed so simple. The person who had broken in and stolen Lash's laptop was the most likely killer.

But the evidence was gone.

Dale had nothing.

31

Dale slipped off his glasses and rubbed his face to soothe his swimming head. The auditorium chair, meant for someone half his size, felt even more uncomfortable. The speaker's rich European-accented voice seemed a distant mumble, incomprehensible.

You're supposed to be smart.

He wasn't smart. Not smart enough.

You're the only one who knows for sure there was a murder. Figure it out.

He wasn't smart enough.

Unless you want to play Video Game Testosterone Hero, your brain is what you've got. Use it.

Dale heaved out a sigh and put his glasses back on.

Someone had removed three key card swipes from the residence hall security system records. Why three?

Maybe the person had broken into three rooms. No, the gaps were widely spaced. One was just after nine AM, the others closer together around two PM.

Two PM! Dale grimaced. He'd forgotten his afternoon ADD pill. He glanced at the time. Three seventeen PM. If he took a pill now, he wouldn't sleep well tonight. If he didn't take a pill now, he'd have even more difficulty coping with the crowd, the talks, all the stimulation of the conference.

Plus he'd have to eat something to keep the pill from making him sick.

There was probably still cake.

The cake pushed his decision. *You're just going to have to be grown-up and deal with the noise. And pay attention. Besides, it's routine stuff that makes you lose focus.*

Today… is not routine.

Dale tightened his mouth.

Assume the killer, the person who broke into the suite and stole Lash's spare laptop deleted the records. That's the one assumption you get. What's the logical question from there?

Dale sucked on his cheek. His mouth tasted like dead eggs. He should have taken the chance to brush—no, focus. The morning atomoxetine hadn't worn off yet, his brain was still working so no excuses, *focus*!

Why delete three records?

Because the intruder… was in a hurry.

Searching through thousands of key swipe records would take time, especially if you weren't familiar with the dataset. Dale had needed a good ten minutes to figure it out, and had needed an outside Perl script to find the missing records.

But telling the records to erase all mention of a particular key card—that was fast. You didn't need much understanding for that, you just say "erase everything for this key card number" and run.

So the killer could be anyone who didn't have a record of a key swipe today.

That still left a whole bunch of people. Dale hadn't swiped his card when he left the suite this morning. But the killer had gone back just after nine.

Maybe he'd wanted to brush his teeth after breakfast?

Then two more missing records, right around two.

The killer had returned to their own room. Maybe they'd paced around. Freaked out. Sobbed into one of those awful pillows.

But somewhere in there, they'd remembered Lash had a backup laptop.

Maybe something on that laptop incriminated the killer.

So the killer had gone to get it.

Dale had almost caught them.

If Dale had been braver, he could have stood still and seen the killer's face.

And if Dale was a soldier, or one of those martial artists, he could have single-handedly taken the killer down. Maybe with a fancy flying kick.

And if Dale was a cop, he could have arrested the killer right there.

And carted them off to lockup tied up across the back of his unicorn.

Back home in Detroit, Dale had seen too many news stories of people killed for being in the wrong place at the wrong time. Idiots who tried to intervene in a mugging got shot. Try to de-escalate an argument, get stabbed.

Running had been right.

Cowardly, but right.

Keep telling yourself that, dude.

Dale shook his head to clear it. What did he know?

Anyone without a record of a key card swipe could be the killer. How many of the conference attendees hadn't swiped in today? Dale ran another query, capturing the data to his laptop. Almost fifteen hundred people in the residence hall. Of those, roughly eight hundred had swiped a key card today.

BSD North had, what, about five hundred attendees? Dale would have to see if conference web site had an attendee list. The other thousand people must be summer students and those high school kids having their tech camps.

The kids were probably sent back to their rooms to brush their teeth after breakfast. And lunch. But who knew how many of them belonged in a room? They were probably stacked twelve to a suite or something.

With so many people not swiping a key card today, the list of seven hundred people who hadn't swiped a card could clear someone's name, but it didn't help Dale build a realistic suspect list.

But…

The killer had been in this system.

They'd needed this system to get into Dale and Lash's suite.

Which meant…

Dale ran another quick query.

Seventy-seven cards had access to every door in the residence halls.

Yesterday, it had been only seventy-four.

Three potential killers.

With names.

32

Never before had a short list made Dale's heart pound.

Bob Matheson

Misha Pokotylo

Dennis Ritchie

Three conference attendees had cards that could get them into any room in the residence halls. Except one was the old man of the conference, one was only tangentially related to the community, and one had been dead for years.

Bob Matheson, godfather of today's BSD software community. He'd been a computer expert for longer than Dale had been alive. When he'd offered the morning's keynote he'd sounded distracted. Uncertain. He'd ended with encouraging words. Dale had put it down to natural discomfort at Lash falling over dead only the hour before… but maybe he'd had more personal reasons for being so shaky?

Pokotylo, from ShufflSoft. He was pretty sexist, yeah, but that didn't make him a killer. He'd attended to talk about ShufflSoft's hooks into, what was it… SkyBSD's filesystem, that was it. A neat feature, sure, but it wouldn't bring him into conflict with Lash. Lash worked in the virtual filesystem layer, well beneath anything Pokotylo touched. While Pokotylo's work used interfaces Lash maintained, interface changes were an annoying fact of life in computing, not cause for murder. Plus, the SkyBSD VFS layer had been pretty stable for years now.

And Dennis Ritchie had been one of the inventors of the Unix operating system, back in the sixties and seventies. Today's geeks might have been pretty smart, but Ritchie had written an operating system on a computer that didn't even have a monitor. If Ritchie wanted to see his work, he'd needed to fire up one of those big monster printers that ran so loudly he might as well have run down the hall trumpeting *I've hit the limits of my brain!* The story was, he hadn't needed to do that often.

Ritchie's Unix was the direct ancestor of BSD. A dozen other operating systems had either been built out of it or directly emulated it, from cellphones to Internet servers. He was literally one of the creators of the modern world.

He'd also died in 2011.

But *Dennis Ritchie* was exactly the sort of pseudonym a computer geek might claim. It would be safely anonymous in the outside world—normal people didn't care about computing history.

But here, amidst a horde of computing professionals, it was perhaps the most foolish pseudonym one could pick.

Dennis Ritchie didn't appear in the residence hall's registration list. The card didn't appear elsewhere in the system.

Some hacker had picked up an extra card somewhere. Maybe one of the teenagers attending camp had dropped theirs, and he'd picked it up. Gone into the system and made it a super-privileged card.

Dale grimaced, wishing he'd thought up the same idea.

But a killer might really, *really* want a pseudonym.

So he had two names, and the mysterious pseudonymous possessor of card number 87153.

While he was in the system, though, he needed to make some changes of his own.

He raised the list of cards that could open any door in the building. The thirty-fourth entry on that list was the number of his old card. If he was going to substitute the number of his new card in its place, this was the time.

Dale found himself hesitating.

He'd never used that type of access before. It's not that he got a kick out of sneaking into other people's private spaces. That access was only a security blanket against the overwhelming pressure of the impenetrable crowds and conversations that filled the world. Every time he left his home or his office, he felt the pressure of people's attention between his shoulder blades. He could feel them, seeing right through him, exposing his every thought, even though they weren't worth being secret.

Everybody could see that he didn't fit in.

He knew it was silly.

He knew everybody felt like that. Maybe not as often as he did, or as strongly, but it was one of those common human experiences.

But that knowledge didn't make the feeling evaporate.

Actually using that access, though… that had changed everything.

Yes, he'd had good reason. A thief, a *killer,* was chasing him.

Dale was not the kind of person to single-handedly confront a murderer. He wasn't the sort of person to single-handedly confront a jaywalker.

But with his hands hovering over the keyboard, ready to super-charge his new key card, Dale felt…

Embarrassed.

He'd violated someone else's privacy.

Not badly, no. He hadn't poked through their belongings. It's not like he'd busted into someone's Google account and gone rummaging.

But he'd stood in someone else's space.

He had a terrible time interacting with people, afraid he was going to screw up, afraid he'd say something that would expose him as not quite normal.

In a way, he'd done to someone else what he feared happening to him.

Even if they never knew it.

His hands trembled over the keyboard.

The new key card in his pocket felt hot enough to burn his thigh.

Dale shifted his hands, leaving the residence hall system unaltered, and disconnected. An invisible weight eased from his chest.

A barrage of applause plunged Dale back into the real world. He blinked, expanding his world from the laptop screen to the lecture hall.

At the front of the room, the CoreBSD speaker raised a hand in appreciation and began packing up his laptop.

Somehow Dale had come to a conference and sat through three talks without hearing a word of any one of them.

But the talks weren't that important any more.

He had to find a way to talk to three people, one of whom he only knew by key card number.

Was "Hey, did you poison Lash?" a good way to broach the subject?

33

The conference schedule gave Dale just enough time to get back to his new suite and dump his weighty laptop backpack before dinner. In the last ninety minutes he'd somehow sweated through the clean shirt. Again. He swapped out the software company's flimsy freebie tee for one of the heavy cotton Detroit Network Services ones he'd brought in his suitcase, sat for two minutes to feebly collect the innumerable thoughts spinning through his skull, and marched himself to the elevator. BSD North attendees filtered into the residence hall lobby, every so often achieving critical mass and moving amoeboid-like out the door with calls of "To dinner!" "See you there!" and "Thirty minutes until open bar!" Dale attached himself to one, and followed the shifting horde down the hill, through the throngs of traffic and scurrying pedestrians.

The sun disappeared behind the tall buildings that climbed the flank of Parliament Hill. What had been a nice breeze suddenly picked up a chill that made Dale's arm hair stand on end and put a shiver between his shoulders.

Byward Market mixed the ritzy shops you'd expect from Canada's national capital with establishments you'd expect next to a college. Expensive restaurants shared walls with cheap pubs. Dale's attention caught on a cart selling something called "beaver tails" that smelled both heavenly and amazingly unhealthy. Jewelry shops offered up the sort of thing you'd buy your daughter on a whim right next to emergency gifts for the French ambassador.

The Irish Arms had a cheerfully green sign with a big four-leaf clover in neon next to it. The brick building sat thirty feet back from the road, but they'd erected a tent over the vast sidewalk. Dale recognized many of the figures lined up at the entrance as BSD North attendees. No, this was Canada—they hadn't lined up, they'd *queued*.

Dale found himself in line behind three tiny Japanese-looking men in painfully white shirtsleeves and brilliant red ties, chattering incomprehensibly to each other as they pointed out market stalls and passers-by that intrigued them. A tall, bony woman joined right behind Dale, intent on her conversation with a pale little British-looking guy afflicted with the world's least manly mustache. Dale didn't know anything about rental properties in Portland, Oregon, so he couldn't join the discussion, but at least he understood the words.

The wind surged, its chill slicing through his shirt. Dale hugged himself to hoard the warmth seeping from his exposed arms and face.

The line moved quickly. The same woman who had offered Dale his wristband guarded the entrance. She smiled at the Japanese trio and said "Great to see you," jerking her head to usher them in as she checked something on her clipboard.

Dale stepped up. Blessedly warm air drifted out from the tent entrance. "Uh, hi."

"Name?"

"Dale. Dale Whitehead."

She flipped a page. "There you are. Have fun."

Dale opened his mouth to say something polite, but she was already turning to the people behind him. He was in the way—again.

He nearly leaped into the noisy warmth of the tent just as the woman behind him said, "Dora LaCroix."

Where had he heard that name before?

The Irish Arms had filled the tent space with rough-hewn picnic tables draped in heavy plastic tablecloths. Pole heaters every ten feet or so blasted welcome warmth and a scent of burnt propane. Computer geeks of every color and dress had colonized sections of tables, most deep in friendly discussion. The front of the building itself was open to the street, the bottom of roll-up doors just barely visible from the top of the doorways, with a bar beyond them and a dim cool interior promising more crowd.

The sound of dozens of conversations assaulted Dale's ears, making him want to pull his ears between his shoulders and hunch around himself like a pretend turtle. The soft smell of beer underlaid everything, sliced through with the sharper tangs of whiskey and vodka and who knew what other sort of booze.

And fried, of course. He couldn't ignore the aroma of something dipped in glorious beer batter and deep fried until it smelled heavenly.

Someone bumped into him from behind. "Excuse me," a woman— the tall woman who'd been behind him—said, elbowing past.

Dale leapt in place. He'd stopped without realizing it, blocking the narrow path between the tables. "Sorry!" He glanced around desperately, slipping into a gap behind the receptionists' podium so he could breathe for a moment.

Dora Lacroix. Why did the name bug him?

He really didn't want to be here. The crowd, the noise, everything felt oppressive.

But he had a job to do.

Talk to Bob Matheson and Misha Pokotylo. See why they could have wanted Lash's computer.

Dale straightened, rolling his head on his neck to try to loosen the taut cables running from the crown of his head down his spine. The crowd noise ebbed and rose like storm-crashed waves in Lake Huron.

But when a gap opened in the people coming in, he slipped into the flow and let it carry him towards the bar.

The crowd inside wasn't made of individuals. It felt like a sea of faces, each appearing only for a moment before blurring into the one next to it. Dale slid into a little gap between the wall and a small waist-high table scattered with drained glasses so he could concentrate on finding people he knew, examining one face at a time.

The woman behind the bar was handing out drinks as fast as she could work the taps, somehow maintaining her smile despite the incessant hands waving for her attention. Surge stood by the bar, a beer already in his hand as he spoke intently with a short chubby guy in a button-down shirt. The guy named after geese—no, ducks… Mallard! *Mallard* stood at a high-top table near the dark wooden wall, drawing pictures in the air to illustrate some point for the half-dozen people near him.

Behind the bar, though, the place looked cavernous, with rows of dark wood tables and benches intermittently spot-lit by can lights set in the dark ceilings. A broad flight of stairs swept upstairs, with people already trickling up, presumably in search of quieter spaces.

Dale instinctively wanted to follow the stairs up. Escape the crush of the crowd and the chaotic churn of nameless faces. Claim an empty table. When another group asked if they could share his table he'd say yes. Let them break the ice.

But right then Bob Matheson squeezed out of the crush around the bar, a tall curved beer glass clenched in each hand, and weaved to a half-empty table cradled in the stairwell's curve.

Matheson was on the list of suspects.

Dale straightened his shoulders and marched himself in.

34

Don't look at the people, Dale commanded himself. *Don't study their faces.*

Get a seat. Then look at the four people.

Deep breath. Sound confident, but not too strong. "Mind if I join you?" Not too bad—a little weak, but not terrible.

One of the guys at the table raised a hand in invitation.

Matheson had claimed a round table with a long plushly-padded bench seat nestled into the inner curve of the stairwell and three straight-back wooden chairs in the outer edge. The locale made him looked less like Reliable BSD Godfather and more like Criminal BSD Godfather. The bench had lots of space, but if Dale squeezed in there the next arrival would trap him.

He claimed one of the chairs.

Matheson sat in the middle of the bench, beer in one hand and rubbing his close-shorn scalp with the other. His morning cheer had evaporated, and the calm confidence he'd displayed earlier in the afternoon had crumbled. "Welcome." Matheson's voice had a definite drunken wobble, but Dale really couldn't blame him. "Welcome."

"Thanks." The glossy wooden chair was even worse than those in the lecture halls, its hard, square shape digging straight into Dale's thighs and the straight back making a comfortable slouch impossible. Maybe the owners thought people would buy more beer to kill the pain? "How are you doing?"

"I'm fine." Matheson raised his glass. Somehow, his ridiculously long mustache wasn't soaked with beer. "I'm all fine." Dale had to concentrate to make out the words over the bar noise, but at least nobody had fired up dance music or anything.

"I was supposed to have dinner with him tonight," said the woman next to Matheson. She wore an oversized hockey jersey lettered in Cyrillic and had an Eastern European accent so thick that it should have gotten up and done one of those crazy Russian high-kicking dances all on its own. She looked familiar—when had Dale seen her before? There weren't that many women at BSD North.

"Lots of us were," said the skinny man on the other side, nodding quickly enough that his ridiculously bushy ponytail flopped up and down. "Not tonight, but, like, we were supposed to hit him up for something."

"I'm Quick," said the last man, offering Dale a hand. With his tidy bow tie and neatly parted short hair, he seemed the most formal of the bunch.

Dale shook the man's hand, staring at his face and silently chanting *Quick, Quick*. "Dale. Dale Whitehead."

Matheson said, "How did you know Lash?"

Dale took a breath. "I was his suitemate."

Heads rose around the table. "That's right," said the woman in the hockey jersey.

Dang it, where had Dale seen that woman before? "I've never been here before," Dale said. "Lash, he… he kind of gave me some hints. Told me about the bar last night. Led me to the conference this morning."

"We try to do that," Matheson said. "Put the new speakers in with someone who's been around before. We don't have the resources for a per-speaker coordinator, but having an old hand around helps."

"He helped." Dale nodded slowly. Lash *had* helped him. Dale just hadn't wanted some of that help. He hadn't wanted to know where last night's bar was. He hadn't really been ready to go to the conference this morning.

But Lash had offered introductions and broken some ice for Dale, when he didn't have to. The thought made Dale melancholy.

"He tried to get me to talk to Pete on kernel locking," said the woman in the jersey. Weirdly, her thick accent made her easier to understand against the background hubbub. "Said we should get a beer and hammer things out."

That discussion felt familiar to Dale as well—the check-in line! That woman had been in line with Lash, right behind Dale. mds@skybsd.org, that was it—but what the hell was her real name?

"For such a nerd, he spent a lot of time getting people to work together," said Quick.

"Someone has to," said the long-haired guy. He hadn't offered a name, so Dale mentally labeled him Mister Ponytail.

MDS—Marina, that was it! Marina, plus a long string of consonants. *Marina* said, "We work together fine. Some people are just wrong."

"Warren would say everybody in the project brings something," said Mister Ponytail.

Marina sighed. "You are right." She slammed the rest of her beer and gave a delicate burp. "I suppose I must go talk to Pete on locking. And try to straighten him out. Things out. Dead man's last request and all."

"Good luck," Dale said. He had to scoot the chair aside to let her slide out of the booth.

"No beer?" said Mister Ponytail, looking at Dale.

"I have to pace myself," Dale said.

Matheson coughed. "I've already paced myself. Paced myself up to the bar, gave the manager a hundred and a card for my hotel, and asked them to pace me out to a cab when I can't see the floor any more."

Dale said, "I guess you knew him pretty well?"

Matheson nodded. "Must be, oh, close to twenty years now. We met... I think it was in BSD Paris, back in the day."

"We met at the Berkeley con," said Quick. "The last one."

"Berkeley isn't what it used to be," said Mister Ponytail. "Can't have a con there."

"Has anything like this happened before?" Dale said.

Matheson shook his head. "We've lost people, sure. The Mad Dane, and Creeping Fuzz, but... never actually at a con." He raised his glass, found it empty, and set it back down with a thud. "Never right at a keynote. I told Langton to order the cheese Danishes because he liked them, you know?" Matheson's alcohol-loosened eyes wandered. "Other people like them, but I thought of him when Ian asked for food suggestions. And he died with one in his hand."

Cheese Danish? Dale frowned. You might not notice almond flavor in a berry Danish, or think twice of it in a plain one, but 'almond and cheese' didn't appear on any Top Ten Flavors list.

Maybe they did in Canada, though. Like gravy and cheese curds.

"Heart attack happens to anyone," Mister Ponytail said.

"Maybe a stroke," Quick said. "The way he swilled coffee, I'd have said a stroke."

"I'm sure we'll hear." Matheson's mustache wobbled with his sudden shudder of distress. "I talked with Lisa—his, his widow." Matheson seemed to be assembling his sentences by hand. If he kept drinking so hard, the manager would call a cab for him before the open bar hour ended.

"How did she take it?" Quick asked.

"The police, they'd already called. She's a wreck. They had two kids. Sad." Matheson peered at his empty glass like it might have grown more beer since he last checked. "So sad. She said… she said she'll let me know what they find out."

Mister Ponytail nodded. "It won't change a thing, but it'd be nice to know."

"Worst bit." Matheson's face seemed to sag. "It's selfish. Really selfish. But Lash, I'd been… teaching him. Someone has to talk to companies. Users. About what we do. I've done this for forty-three years now. About time to let someone else take over. Someone younger. What seems like a great idea at forty-one, at fifty-six… now, not so smart." He raised a hand to cover a belch. "His wife, his daughter, they're in trouble, and I keep thinking that I could be home with my husband, and instead I'm stuck flying around the world being the face of BSD for another year."

Dale winced.

Matheson might have a magic card that let him in any room in the residence hall, but he had a distinct reason for wanting Lash alive.

Then again…

What if Matheson had realized he didn't want to give up being the Godfather of BSD?

Was he broken up because of what he'd lost?

Or because of what he'd done?

35

Speakers in the dark ceiling buzzed. A boisterous voice with a faint French accent announced, "The Irish Arms welcomes BSD North. Our staff will be bringing plates and food out momentarily. Finding a seat would let your *magnifique* feast begin."

"There we go," Mister Ponytail said. "What was the menu, again?"

"Pork roast," Matheson said. "Chicken. Three different potatoes, greens, a couple different salads, cornbroad." He closed his mouth. "Corn. *Bread*. Other bread. Dessert buffet after. And, and… stuff."

"You'll feel better with some food," Quick said.

Matheson just shook his head.

Trying to pique Matheson's interest, Dale said "You'll be able to drink longer with some food."

Mister Ponytail glared hot fury at Dale. "He needs to slow down."

Dale's heart sank. Ponytail was right—Matheson was already soused.

Matheson raised a finger to point unsteadily at Dale. "That man— that is the *truth*. Dale. You're smart. Come back next year, I promise— promise!—nobody will die."

Embarrassment made Dale's face flush. "I'm sure. And some food will help you feel better." Not that food ever made Dale feel better, but it's what people said.

"Don't want to feel better," Matheson said.

"Trust me," Quick said. "Tomorrow morning, you'll feel terrible."

"Good."

Dale's stomach churned. He hated watching people get drunk—yes, at times he himself had downed a couple too many, but that had been accidental, not Matheson's deliberate headlong plunge into the bottle.

Not that Dale could blame him tonight.

Dale had to talk to Pokotylo. See if the man had a motive.

And find out who was walking around with card 87153, owned by "Dennis Ritchie."

But he couldn't just excuse himself from Matheson's obvious distress.

Lash had been popular. Dale had the feeling Matheson wouldn't be the only one doing serious drinking tonight.

A disturbingly perky twenty-something face loomed out of the dim light.

Dale jumped.

"Good evening gentlemen!" The waitress' black shirt and slacks disappeared against the bar's darkness, transforming her into a spooky floating face and hands. She hefted a stack of plates. "Can I slip in here?"

"Waitresses always have right of way," Quick said.

Dale scooted his chair to the side.

The group sat in silence while the waitress dealt eight plates like playing cards. A waiter appeared seconds later, efficiently distributing cutlery wrapped in coarse linen napkins.

Dale gratefully took the chance to think, but his mind whirled in place. Matheson's grief. Ritchie, Pokotylo. Lash's bright red face. A half-eaten cheese Danish tumbling from a dying hand.

The waiter had just disappeared when a voice behind Dale said, "Hey, those seats free?"

Ponytail looked over Dale's head. "Smalls! Blixton! Nah, get in here."

The table filled in moments as everyone looked for a spot to each. Dale found himself sitting between a tiny Italian man with an impressive beard and a tall guy with the lean build of a long-distance runner. A guy shaped roughly like a six-foot-wide basketball squeezed in next to Mister Ponytail, the table squeezing his gut until it flopped over the table.

Names flooded over Dale, gone too quickly for him to try to remember them. He managed to catch that Smalls was the huge guy, but knew he'd only remember that because Smalls wasn't small. Thankfully the food arrived before anyone noticed Dale's ignorance.

Breakfast had been institutional.

Lunch had been okay.

But when the relay team of waiters set massive platters in the middle of the table, the smells of gently seasoned roast pork and grilled chicken marinated in balsamic vinegar reached right up Dale's nose and into his brain.

He felt proud of himself for skipping the afternoon cake.

The loud sound of voices dropped around them, gradually replaced with a lower murmur of conversation and the clatter of cutlery.

Dale avoided having to talk by the simple technique of taking one bite after another. He tried to cut the meat into small bits and chew each thoroughly, but the tender pork dissolved on his tongue. The roasted potatoes and multi-colored carrots tasted of garlic and rosemary, and he'd never had a salad quite like the little beans in vinegar sauce.

Dale kept his ears open as he ate, concentrating on the discussion.

Quick diverted Matheson from his musings on Lash, getting him to talk about how he ran BSD North and then steering him into the delights of the many places he'd traveled. Matheson kept touching on his memories of Lash at other conferences, but only the happier ones. Trying to flush the toilet in a Japanese hotel without summoning the police. Touring dockside at BSD Malta back in '09, where a standing sign outside a canopy said lunch special, but special with two s's, for two, three kinds of fish "caught by my husband this morning," but it was really five kinds of fish, and these tiny bottles of African beer you could down like popcorn.

But the ramblings broke Matheson's gloom and gave him a chance to sober up a touch.

Dale focused on Matheson's words, listening for some slip that would prove the man's guilt or innocence. That's how the greats did it, catching some little slip the killer made. The only thing Dale discovered in Matheson's words was genuine grief.

Dale made himself stop after a second serving of the delectable pork roast. He eyed the potatoes, but he'd already had two small halves, plus the grilled veggies, plus a bit of all three salads. He didn't need any more carbs tonight, at all.

His stomach felt full. He really didn't need any more.

But that grilled chicken smelled fantastic.

Matheson stopped talking long enough to stuff another forkful of pork in his mouth.

To distract himself from the meal Dale said, "It sounds like you get everywhere."

Matheson nodded, chewing. He fumbled for the beer glass, but found it still empty.

Quick said, "If you're a good speaker, you can go just about anywhere."

Matheson hurriedly swallowed. "That's the trick." He coughed into his fist. "See, if you're an expert on something, you can get a speaking slot at one of the more local cons. But once people know who you are, you can submit to talks all over. The con pays airfare, hotel, and you get them to delay your return for a couple days. You pay those hotel days, sure. The con gets sponsors to pay for travel, so you're pretty much flying on Google or Microsoft's dime, or one of the Foundations, and they get their money from the big guys." Matheson raised his fork to point at Dale. "You, sir—next year, wait to go home. See some of Ottawa. Parliament Hill. Diefenbunker. There's cheap hotels, like, Chinatown, or Little Italy. Get some poutine."

"Poutine," groaned the massive Smalls. "Don't remind me."

Dale had avoided poutine, a good candidate for Canada's national dish. Certainly fresh-cooked, fresh-cut fries covered with cheese curds and gravy would taste heavenly, but just smelling the stuff would put him up a shirt size.

Quick said, "Donner keeps threatening to be the BSD North poutine sponsor."

"Jerk," Smalls said. His gaze seemed glued to the pork roast platter. *Keep your hands off your fork, or you'll end up like that poor bastard.*

"It will not happen," said the tiny Italian man next to Dale. "He is completely talk. That is why he writes books instead of doing real code."

No, bread doesn't need a fork. Don't touch it either.

"Poutine at the con would be fun," Matheson said. "But Byward's not really set up for outside catering. Not many poutineries around that can handle five hundred people."

Fresh cut fries sounded good. Dale didn't have to get the cheese curds and gravy.

"Their school kitchen must do poutine," said the Italian.

But if Dale was in Ottawa, he should try poutine. Ottawa was right up against Quebec, the home of poutine. He wouldn't be back here again. It was a once-in-a-lifetime chance.

"The school's poutine is awful," Mister Ponytail said. "Just awful."

"Not that bad," said Quick.

Dale relaxed. If he was going to have that once-in-a-lifetime meal, he wanted the best. So long as he didn't know where to get it—

"We need to get you to Smokey's, right across the street," Mister Ponytail said. "You'll never touch lesser poutine again."

Dammit!

"I need something to drink," Dale said. "Anyone else?"

"Open bar has ended," said the Italian.

Inspiration hit Dale. "I can't get everyone," Dale said, "but my boss said to buy drinks for people."

Faces perked up around the table. "Well, *we* aren't everyone," Smalls said. "We're just the important people."

"Maybe." He wanted to know who had card 87153. Dale fumbled in his pocket, to drag out his key card, and held it up as if studying the number faintly embossed on it. Hurried math churned in his brain— no, it's not divisible by two, obviously, but maybe three… "My key card is number is… 29051. If your card number is a multiple of that, a factor of that, or… or if it's a prime number, drinks are on me."

Before he finished, hands were reaching into wallets to read off key card numbers.

Dale let himself give a little smile. Drinks and math caught a geek every time.

I will find you, Mister "Ritchie."

36

Nobody at the table had 87153, or any other multiple of 29051, but the Italian guy had a prime—78317. The others congratulated him, more than one calling him Max. Dale studied his face, silently chanting *Max Max Max* as the others encouraged him to try the Napoleonic cognac or maybe see if the bar had some of that rare Etruscan 1821 vintage. Max waved them off and asked for a Blue.

The crowd around the bar wasn't nearly as thick as it had been before dinner. Dale managed to grab a Labatt's Blue for Max and, after a thought, a lime and tonic for himself.

Dale didn't mind drinking. If he was to have any hope of identifying Lash's killer, though, he needed the clearest head he could manage.

The crowd's ongoing grumble abraded Dale's nerves, creating a dull ache behind his eyes. Without his afternoon meds, the noise hit him like a herd of tiny elephants trampling from the crown of his head right down his spine and back. When someone spoke Dale not only had to concentrate on their words, he needed to painstakingly assemble the sounds into words and the words into a sentence. Even with the atomoxetine, the noise would have strained his senses.

The brief round of applause when he returned with Max's drink didn't improve things. Max accepted his beer with a smile.

"So," Mister Ponytail said. "Are you going to be buying drinks all night?"

"If people have the right number, sure." Dale thought quickly. "But don't tell people what the game is. Just say I'm buying drinks for certain card numbers."

If Dale could get numbers from a whole bunch of people, he could rule them out as suspects. Making the rounds and talking to people would wear him out—no, it would exhaust him. But if he could find out who *wasn't* carrying the Dennis Ritchie card, it would be worth it.

"That's a great icebreaker," Quick said. "Wish I'd thought of it."

The wreckage of the dinner feast lay across the table. Dale could still taste the pork. If he sat down, he could have another piece or two. The wait staff had already brought refills—he could have a whole pig if he wanted.

If Dale sat, he was finished.

No—the food would be finished, Dale would just be starting.

Max raised his Blue to salute Dale, then downed half the beer in a single impressive gulp.

Dale took a sip of the tonic, rolling it around his mouth to wash away some of the taste of dinner. "I need to talk to some folks," he said. "If you'll excuse me?"

The table chorused farewells as Dale turned to study the room.

Most people had finished dinner, but still lurked over devastated platters of vegetables and meat. A few folks stood in the small spaces at the head of the tables, drinks in hand, busily talking with others, but Dale didn't recognize any of them.

He couldn't just stand there. The people back at Matheson's table would catch on that he had finished with them.

No, they didn't know he had an ulterior goal. They'd probably think that he just wanted to get away from them.

That wasn't any better.

The stairs. If he wasn't walking straight towards anyone, at least he could get out of sight for a moment. Maybe a thinner crowd. A *quieter* one. A little more space would be nice.

After the dark main floor, the comparatively bright upper floor made Dale blink. Half a dozen dinner tables sat lined up near the stairs, but the space beyond was an open dance floor surrounded by great big windows showing off the spectacular view of Byward Market. A few clusters of people stood around the dance floor, deep in conversation.

He'd gotten away. Now how to get into a conversation?

Pokotylo had seemed friendly enough. If Dale saw him he could just walk past and say hi. But to find out who had the Dennis Ritchie card, he had to talk to a whole bunch of people. Explain his numbers game.

He had to inject himself into conversations, again and again.

The same problem he'd had all his life.

Dale let out a despairing breath and slowly walked to the closest window. The sun had vanished, but the skies gleamed gold and red over the buildings climbing Parliament Hill, fading towards deep blue overhead. Below, the streets were even more crowded. In the time since he'd arrived at the Irish Arms, pedestrians had overrun the streets of Byward Market, reducing the few cars to creeping. Some kind of busker had claimed the open space near the parking garage, and was making a big deal out of her coat—was that a straitjacket? And why did she have that big propane ring? How'd she get it to raise four foot flames?

Going down to watch the show might be entertaining. And he could get back in, he had his wristband. Loud, yes, and the crowd looked that indifferent sort of pushy, but he'd be anonymous.

Dale shook his head.

If he didn't figure out who murdered Lash, nobody ever would.

Staring out the window felt peaceful.

He made himself turn back into the crowd.

Near the middle of the dance floor, someone waved.

Dale needed a moment to sort out Surge's face from all the others around him.

In that moment, Surge nodded and waved again.

You wanted in a conversation. Okay, not wanted—needed.

Dale straightened and walked over.

"Dale," Surge said, turning away from the half-dozen people in his conversation.

"Surge."

"I got your patches in the test cluster two hours ago."

Patches? Oh, right. When someone had stolen Lash's computer, Dale had forgotten his carefully constructed improvements to SkyBSD. "And?"

"The cluster hasn't crashed yet."

"Er… good?"

One side of Surge's face cocked up in a smile. "That's better than most patch sets do, actually. The test suite should be done tomorrow morning. I'll let you know the results. You've caused a whole bunch of talk, actually."

Talk? Worry flickered in Dale's brain. "What's to talk about?"

"The test lab is great. Ten gig, forty gig switches, all sorts of different network interfaces and physical media. The problem is, your patches specifically address crappy networks." Surge shrugged. "We don't have a crappy network to test them on."

Dale relaxed. They hadn't talked about him, not really. "I'm sure if you ask around, you can find a bunch of us to help you out there."

"I'm sure. This patch set, though." Surge nodded. "It's the one I'm interested in, but it turns out you've sent a bunch of patches in. Even something in NFS 4?"

No, they *had* talked about him. "Only when I hit problems."

"That's how we all get started. You keep doing that and we'll have to give you a commit bit."

Not again. "Isn't that a bit premature?"

Surge shrugged. "It's better than me committing all these patches for you."

One of the people in the conversation turned to face Surge. "You know, if we ran Git, that wouldn't be a problem. One click and done."

Surge rolled his eyes. "The Git thing isn't going to happen."

"Git is vile," said a tall, gaunt woman. She'd been in line behind Dale to check in for dinner. LaCroix, that was it—Dora LaCroix.

Dale had a sudden flashback to Peterson saying *We might as well get T-shirts that say Team LaCroix or Team Hellman*. This woman had been arguing with Jason Hellman online, an argument that sparked Lash's efforts to create a SkyBSD harassment policy.

He'd heard hints that Lash wanted to put some rules in place to prevent harassment. Hearsay wasn't evidence, but Dale had no idea who to talk to for better insight. And theoretically, LaCroix would be in favor of a policy against sexual harassment.

But the only way to find out for sure was to talk to her.

37

Dinner had had time to settle, leaving Dale feeling a little too full. If he tripped, he might pop. At least he hadn't eaten until his stomach hurt, though. The meal's comforting weight would normally make him drowsy, but the rising and ebbing crowd noise surging up the stairwell kept his shoulders clenched.

He really wanted to go back to his room.

Or back to Detroit.

But Surge had drawn him into a conversation. Dale needed to take advantage of that.

The Git fan was a middle-aged guy with a shock of prematurely white hair and skin so pale the veins of his face were visible even under the bar's can lights. His dark T-shirt and jeans made him look even more pale. "Lash was the one who put the kibosh on Git."

"Not just him," Surge said.

"The Senate was split five-to-four Subversion," the Git fan said. His BSD North name badge fluttered around his neck. Dale squinted and caught the last name: Smith. "And Lash did the original CVS-to-Subversion migration. He knew Subversion, like, carnally."

LaCroix said, "So you're saying, with Lash dead you Git fans have a chance?"

Smith raised his hands. "No, no, no! Lash was cool. I didn't agree with him, but that's why we elect the Senate."

"They'll have an election for his replacement," Surge said.

A beefy guy on the other side of LaCroix said, "Nope. No election until the Senate falls to five members."

"You sure?" Surge said.

"I just read the SkyBSD bylaws," the beefy guy said. "Emergency election is called when the Senate falls to five. Empty spaces are filled in order of time remaining on the term, based on total votes. Whoever gets the most votes gets the longest partial term."

If Lash died because he opposed Git, the killer needed to take out one more SkyBSD Senate member who hated Git. The cold practicality of the thought embarrassed Dale. But if someone else died in the near future…

"Right," LaCroix said. "That means the pro-Git forces need to take out one more Senate member to shift the balance."

Dale felt his face heat at LaCroix voicing his secret thought.

Surge glared at LaCroix. "Lash died right in front of us, Dora. It's… That's a pretty damn tasteless thing to say."

LaCroix stiffened. Her jaw set. Anger spun behind her eyes. She looked ready to take a swing.

Dale tensed. Should he get between them? How ugly would this get?

LaCroix said stiffly, "Lash was my friend. He wouldn't mind me joking about him."

"Warren was my friend too," Surge said. "I've given my whole life to SkyBSD, to the community, *for* the community. I've built a whole bunch of the tools we use, especially the stuff for our Subversion workflow. Lash and I, we defined how SkyBSD's commit process works. Once we start saying someone murdered him, even *joking* about it, the whole community blows apart. Right now, we need to hold together."

LaCroix studied Surge.

Dale held his breath.

"Warren died by accident," LaCroix said. "It's ridiculous to say anything else, seriously."

Dale let his breath go.

"He turned that bright red," Smith said. "Isn't that a cyanide—"

"Or a heart attack," Surge interrupted. "Or a bunch of other things. Hypertension. He dealt with enough social crap to raise anybody's blood pressure."

"And what's *that* supposed to mean?" LaCroix snapped.

Dale's breath caught again.

Surge lifted his empty hand, palm towards LaCroix. "The Senate gets all the stuff nobody else wants to deal with. And Warren took on the worst of it. If I had that gig, my blood pressure would be through the roof."

LaCroix's face got a little redder as her bony jaw tightened further. Her argument with Hellman had been one of the problems Lash had taken on. She not only looked ready to take a swing at Surge, she seemed prepared to knock him to the floor and kick him in the head.

A restaurant this size must have security people. Or maybe a couple big waiters? Would they notice? Or did management just call the cops when a fight broke out?

"If you'll excuse me," LaCroix said, "I need to go drink a toast for my friend."

She wheeled away to stalk to the stairwell.

The beefy guy let out a breath. "She sure don't like you, does she?"

"We always got along before," Surge said. "It's this harassment policy."

Suspicions fluttered in the back of Dale's brain. He pondered how to phrase the question without flat-out saying *What did you think of the policy?*

"We need something to do when someone starts being a dick," Smith said.

"People are dicks," Surge said. "The Internet was built on being a dick."

"So you're good with people going after a woman?" the beefy guy said.

"I didn't say that," Surge said. "That's crap behavior, sure. If someone's a jerk, call them a jerk, you don't need sexist language. Or racist. Whatever. Making big complicated rules for how to behave, though—that doesn't work."

"What's wrong with rules against harassment?" the beefy guy said.

Surge rolled his eyes. "Rules exist to be exploited. Evaded. To make a rule against harassment, you have to define it. A real, dedicated jerk, though—they'll dance right up around the edges of the definition and make it impossible to do anything about them. What we need right now is someone to tell those two—" he jerked a thumb at LaCroix's head disappearing down the stairwell "—to cool it."

"There's no requirement to behave," Smith said.

"It's in the committer's handbook," Surge said. "Right in the first paragraph. We're expected to be civil to each other."

"Whoever wrote that never saw IRC," the beefy guy said.

"Still," Surge said. "It's in there. If they want a rule to enforce, there it is. The hard part is doing it. There's no policy in the world that can make someone not be a dick. Besides, this whole thing is a distraction."

"Distraction?" Dale said.

"Sure," Surge said. "LaCroix, Hellman, they don't commit enough to be worth putting much effort into. Couple commits a month, each. They got into a fight and couldn't settle it like adults? Throw them both out."

Dale grimaced. Someone had stolen naked pictures of LaCroix and posted them on the Internet. If that had happened to him—well, first, someone would have to *take* that kind of picture, and nobody was even vaguely interested in that gig. Still, exposing someone like that was a couple levels above mere jerkdom. It'd make him pretty angry.

But the story was that friends of Hellman's had done exactly that.

Was Hellman responsible for his friends' actions? Dale couldn't see how.

If Hellman had defended them, though, LaCroix had every right to get mad. Not just mad: eye-gouging furious. She shouldn't be kicked out of a community over standing up for herself.

Smith said, "So they're committers because nobody felt like handling their patches for them?"

"Pretty much," Surge said.

"You know," Smith said, "Git's patch merging makes that whole problem go away."

"Oh, shut up," Surge rolled his eyes again, harder, then stomped off.

162

38

Dale wasn't going to trail after Surge like a lost puppy, but uncomfortable silence filled the space between him, Smith, and the beefy guy.

"So," the beefy guy said. "My name's Dean. Dean Leslie."

"Dale," Dale said.

"Dale." Smith offered a hand. "I'm Uri Smith."

"Nice to meet you," Dale said. There, a conversation was moving, sort of.

"What do you think of the whole Git thing?" Smith said.

Dale shrugged. "I'm not part of SkyBSD, just a user. How they run it is their choice." *That's a great way to keep a conversation going, dude. Are you* trying *to drive it into a ditch?*

"Surge sounded like he wanted to bring you in," Leslie said.

"I can't see that happening," Dale said. "It's nice, but—no."

"Haven't seen you here before," Leslie said. "Your first time?"

"Yep," Dale said. "I'm talking about wireless tomorrow morning."

"Don't mind Surge and Dora." Leslie rubbed his big meaty hands together. "Dora's taking all this pretty personal, and with Warren this morning…"

"Yeah," Dale said.

Smith said, "On that note, I'm passing the word along. The charity auction tomorrow, at the closing session? We vote on the charity at lunch. Someone came up with the idea of a Warren Lash Memorial Fund. Raise some money for his family."

"Nice idea," Dale said.

"Didn't he have life insurance?" Leslie said.

Dale blinked. What kind of jerk cared if Lash had life insurance? His family was hurting—

Leslie said, "No, wait, that's premature optimization talking, never mind. It's a great idea, we should do it."

"Glad you think so," Smith said stiffly.

"I'll mention it," Dale said.

"Thanks."

The conversation died. A second of silence.

Two seconds.

Dale fought to keep his teeth from clenching. "Hey, you want to win a free drink?"

"What is this, a sales pitch?" Leslie said.

"No," Dale said. "My boss said to buy drinks. I can't get everyone, so I have a game. What's the number on your room key?"

"They have a number?" Smith dug in his pocket.

"Pretty sure they—oh, you're at the university," Leslie said. "I'm staying at the Comfort Inn around the corner."

Smith extracted a pale white Byward University residence hall key card from his wallet.

"What's the number?" Dale said.

"What's the game?" Smith said.

"Is it prime?" Dale said. "Or a multiple of 29051?"

"Why 29051?" Leslie said.

"My key number."

"Cool." Smith narrowed his eyes to peer at the card. "I'm… 86121."

"Could be prime," Leslie said, whipping out his phone. "Let's see. 86121…"

Dale really needed to take a moment and hook his phone up to the bar's Internet so he could grab a list of five-digit primes. Dinking with his phone was a lot more comfortable than talking to people, though.

If he started poking at the tiny screen, he might not realize how much time had passed until the battery died or the bar closed. 86121 was odd, so two was out, try three—

"Nope," Smith said. "Divisible by three."

Leslie tapped at his phone a couple more times. "Yep."

It was his idea, and they'd done the math first. Embarrassed, Dale divided furiously. "And, uh, 12,303. And seven."

"So, do I owe *you* a drink now?" Smith said.

Leslie chuckled.

"I knew I forgot something," Dale said. "I'll add that rule next time."

"Hey George," Leslie said to a person in a separate discussion right behind him. "What's your key card number?"

Dale had spent his whole life jumping up and down to try to break conversational ice, but all of a sudden the ice shattered beneath him and plunged him into an icy lake of faces and voices. People eagerly offered up card numbers, and within a few minutes Dale found himself walking back down to the bar to buy a petite Indian man a shot of Grey Goose. Dale had to deliberately concentrate on the face and voice of the person directly in front of him, hurriedly sieving words from the jabbering crowd and rushing to assemble them into coherent sentences before the person realized that Dale hadn't understood.

For the most part, he managed. The couple times he didn't understand, holding a hand to his ear made people talk more loudly and slowly. That made the bar's noise worse, but gave him the numbers he needed.

He wasn't finding the pseudonymous Dennis Ritchie.

But he was identifying a whole bunch of people who weren't Dennis Ritchie. Just as he'd hoped.

Sadly, they appeared and evaporated so quickly that he didn't have even a chance of remembering their names or their faces.

He should have made a list. No, then he really would have looked like a sales drone and nobody would have talked to him.

And sooner or later, he'd roll into his other named suspect, Pokotylo.

A few minutes after Dale began taking numbers *en masse*, Hellman appeared.

Dale couldn't help tensing. Hellman and LaCroix's argument had raised Lash's blood pressure, if nothing else. And Lash had wanted to put rules in place against the way Hellman had behaved.

And Hellman knew where to find the cyanide.

In Dale's mind, that made Hellman suspect number one.

But Hellman's card number was 19546. He wasn't Ritchie.

Hellman shrugged and drifted back into the crowd.

Dale bought drinks for four prime numbers before someone stepped right into his face and bellowed "Roomie!"

Dale blinked and recoiled from the thinly bearded chin that had appeared right in front of his eyes.

Rob Deck, his new suitemate, had an empty beer mug in one hand. "Dale, right?"

"Yeah," Dale said. "What's your key card number?"

"I heard about that." Deck's belch was surprisingly delicate for such a big, boisterous guy. "Great idea, but I'm on expense account."

Dale's suspicions flared. Had he changed suites only to wind up with one of the suspects? No, Deck had been with Dale when Dale said he was going back to his room. Deck wouldn't have tried to steal Lash's laptop right when he knew Dale would be there. Not even a brainy computer geek was *that* dumb.

"Besides," Deck said, "It's not a prime number, ends in two and starts in one, so it's not a multiple of two nine whatever you have." He leaned closer. "You seen Surge around?"

Dale glanced at the stairwell. "Uh, he was upstairs last I saw him." What did a high-level CoreBSD hacker want with a SkyBSD hacker?

Deck shook his head. "Nah, not anymore." He frowned, expression meandering between dubious and angry. "I'll catch that bastard at breakfast tomorrow. Probably nothing anyway. Listen." He covered his mouth to divert another belch. "Me and a bunch of the CoreBSD guys, we're heading out on the Pub Crawl of Doom. Interested? Nine pubs in Byward Market, and we're gonna drink at every one of them."

Dale blinked. "That's… a lot of beer."

Deck waved his arms. "There's a lot of me. And I've done a lot of VFS hacking. I thought the IP stack was bad, but VFS makes hard drinking mandatory. How about it?"

Some of the top CoreBSD developers in the world were at BSD North. An invitation to hang out with them was something to grab with both hands.

But Deck was clearly a better drinker than Dale.

And Dale had a murderer to find. He couldn't do that barfing in a gutter.

"I talk first thing," Dale said. "Can I get a rain check?"

"Sure." Deck leaned in closer. "Listen, what happened to Warren, don't let it get to you. Not your fault."

Not my fault, but I guess it's my responsibility. "Thanks."

"You see Surge," Deck said as he turned away, "you tell him I'm looking for him."

Deck had been polite this afternoon, but with a few drinks in him he became larger than life. So much larger, than just being in the same room with him made Dale feel crowded.

Deck weaved into the tent fronting the building and out onto the sidewalk.

If Dale left now, he could get back to the residence hall well before Deck returned. He could shower in peace. Have an hour of quiet before bed. Read a little. Let his whirligig thoughts settle out.

He could end the painful labor of talking to all these people.

But once the conference ended, everyone would disperse. Even when the police figured out Lash really had been poisoned, they'd never get all the suspects together again.

Dale's shower wouldn't be peaceful if he gave up on finding Lash's killer.

And right there, through a gap in the crowd, he saw Pokotylo. Named suspect number two.

Dale drained the last of his tonic and lime, set the glass on a litter-choked tray, and marched himself forward.

39

Pokotylo, sitting with a couple of older men at one end of a long table right next to the Irish Arms' central bar, raised a glass half-full of thick foamy dark beer as Dale approached. "Ah, our newest ShufflSoft committer! Your bug reports, they are closed, no?"

Dale had to concentrate to assemble Pokotylo's words into meanings. "Not yet. It's been a rough day." Talking to everyone, even with the excuse of his numbers trick, had worn his nerves paper-thin. His head felt two sizes too big, the extra space filled with gluey tar that squeezed his brain.

"Yes." Pokotylo turned to the others and raised his glass again. "To Warren Lash."

The other men raised their glasses. "Lash."

That wasn't too hard to understand. Dale had heard the sounds of Lash's name often enough tonight that they had remained familiar.

"Sit, Dale, sit." Pokotylo wobblily waved at the empty stretch of bench. "You have no drink?"

"Been drinking all night." Tonic water and lime was a drink. "I need to cool it a bit." Dale's joints ached too, as if the headache had bled into his knees and hips and shoulders and even his fingers. If he had a beer now, he might sit down and never stand again.

"Is not a night for cooling it," Pokotylo said. "The BSD family, they lost one of their own, no? Is a night for serious drinking. For waking up in your own puke with a head size of angry bulldozer and knowing you don't hurt as much as his wife. We drink for *respect*." He raised his glass. "Sláinte—that's right, no?"

The guy with the monstrous beard sitting across from Pokotylo raised his glass. "I."

Dale stopped. *I?* Shouldn't the guy have said more than that? Or was he losing whole chunks of words now?

Pokotylo drained a swallow and pointed at the bearded man. "Dale, this is Andy, he's a real Irishman. From Ireland. And over there... I'm sorry."

The third man, yet another chubby bald guy in a T-shirt, held out a hand to Dale. "Jack."

"Dale." Jack's hand felt hot and sweat-sticky. Dale smelled the booze in his sweat even across the table.

"Right," Pokotylo set his glass back on the table. "Tomorrow, my head, too big for commits. You have trouble, IRC, no?"

"Sure," Dale said. "Hey, what's your key card number?"

None of the three had Ritchie's card, nor even a prime number. The gambit got Dale into the group, though. He wished he'd thought of buying his way into conversations years ago.

"You need drink," Pokotylo said.

"Really, I've had enough," Dale said.

"No such thing," Pokotylo said.

"Let him be," one of the guys—Joe? No, Jack, that was it—said. "At a table with a Russian and an Irishman?"

"Ukraine!" Pokotylo said.

"Ukraine, fine." Jack waved a hand. "A Ukrainian and an Irish… Irish… Irishian? The poor guy can't hope to keep up with *this* table."

The Irish guy raised his glass. "Canna argue with that."

"Skoal." Pokotylo tapped his glass to Andy's.

"Any of you know Lash?" Dale said. "Warren?"

"Not a bit," Pokotylo said cheerfully.

"I," said the Irishman again. No, wait—*aye*, not I.

"Yeah," Jack said. "He helped me with some VFS patches. Mentored me when I got my commit bit."

Pokotylo and the Irish guy both hoisted their glasses at that. Dale pushed his brain, trying to remember the Irishman's name. He'd just heard it, *just* heard it, but the noises and faces and everything had just about overwhelmed him.

"You know what you must do," Pokotylo slurred. "You mentor another."

"Two more," the Irishman—Andy, that was it.

Dale tried to make himself study Andy's face. He seemed normal enough, but his features refused to fit into Dale's brain.

Jack raised his glass. "Not yet. I'm not nearly good enough to mentor."

"Nobody is ever good enough," Pokotylo said. "But together—ah, together! Together, we change world, da?" He nodded at Dale. "Dale here. He do good work, on little piece of ShufflSoft. We bring him in, and maybe he take on more. Maybe he expands web framework. Together, we take out Drupal."

"That's the hard bit," Jack said. "SkyBSD's a lot bigger than ShufflSoft. Warren did a lot to hold us together. He worked hard to settle fights."

"Bah!" Pokotylo rolled his eyes. "People fight, you send them outside into street. Maybe take bets."

"Keep thinking that, and ShufflSoft won't get much bigger," Jack said.

Pokotylo said, "SkyBSD settle problems their way. We settle, our way." He leaned forward. "Who cares, my friend? Some girl can't stand up for herself, who cares?"

Dale's tongue felt thick. He felt like saying that he cared, but how would he follow that up? What would the conversation turn into?

No, he was overthinking this. Try simpler:

What would Peterson say?

Dale took a deep breath. "Sometimes you have to tell someone that they're being a jerk. For, say, putting up naked pics of someone."

"You too? Bah!" Pokotylo drowned the rest of his beer.

Dale tensed. What do you think he going to do, mister? Take a swing at you?

But Pokotylo only shouted "More beer! My round, no?"

Dale relaxed.

Andy drained his glass. "Another lager, please."

Jack said something—what was it? No, he put his palm over the mouth of his glass too. He must have said some kind of *no*.

"Your loss." Pokotylo turned. Dale focused his gaze on the man's mouth as he spoke, trying to piece the sounds together into words. "Dale? You're" *something* "serious. Need beer."

Now he was really losing words. Not good.

If Dale put a beer on top of his overstimulated brain, he'd probably wake up tomorrow morning across the river in Hull, in a gutter, with no idea how he got there, and a hit squad of livid Québécois mobsters after him. He needed to finish this and go back to his room.

Besides, Dale's impressions couldn't conclusively clear Pokotylo. Dale wasn't ready to drink anything he hadn't gotten from the bar himself. "Thanks, but I'm done for tonight."

If one of the people at the table fell over dead, though, he'd know who the killer was.

If Pokotylo's eyes rolled any harder they would have fallen out of his head. "*Americans.*"

Andy shook his head sadly and leaned towards Dale. Somehow, he made his words penetrate the crowd without raising his booze-laden voice. Maybe it was the accent. "You come to BSD Belfast. We'll teach you how to drink properly."

An eight-hour plane ride? The thought froze Dale's blood. "I just might do that."

Pokotylo wove towards the bar.

Dale closed his eyes, trying to think.

Pokotylo toasted Lash's memory, but didn't seem to care enough about him to kill him. Dale had the impression Pokotylo considered Lash's death an excuse to get really, really drunk.

That left the only suspect as the mysterious Dennis Ritchie. The hunt for Ritchie had exhausted Dale.

A thread of satisfaction underlay Dale's frustrated hunt, though.

If the conference was divided into Team Hellman and Team LaCroix, he'd declared himself for a side. Weakly, yes, but more than he'd ever managed before.

And Pokotylo had changed the topic. He'd gone to buy a round rather than respond.

Pokotylo had backed down.

Dale felt pretty good about that.

Dale waited for Pokotylo to return with the drinks, then excused himself for the men's room. The tonic-and-limes had had their effect, but they were just an excuse to depart before Pokotylo made another uncomfortable sexist comment. Dale didn't want to know how bad the guy would be with all that booze on board.

The bathroom clock said almost ten-thirty.

Dale didn't have much more time to find Ritchie.

Already, the countless faces he'd ruled out blurred in his memory. Someone could say, "Thanks for the drink," and Dale would have no idea who he was, or if he'd actually bought him a drink or not.

Ruling out suspects? No, he'd only worn himself out.

Leaving the bathroom, the Irish Arms felt a little emptier. Was that an echo on the dark-paneled walls?

His opportunity to find Ritchie evaporated with the evening. Dale shook his hands to get the last of the water off.

His hands felt strange at the ends of his wrists, like the screws holding his bones together had started to come loose.

Dale looked.

His fingers had an extra tremor.

Dale stopped, trying to still his whirling brain.

Too many people. Too many faces. Too many words.

And too much damned attention deficit disorder.

Pretty soon, he wouldn't be able to understand anything *anyone* said. Tonight would have been rough even with the afternoon atomoxetine.

Without it, he was done.

He hadn't found Dennis Ritchie yet.

If he walked away, Lash's murderer would escape cleanly.

But Dale's brain had finally reached the inevitable ADD crash.

If he didn't stop soon—*really* soon, even a night's sleep wouldn't fix him.

Dale was done.

40

Even the dimly lit bar's thinning crowd pressed in on Dale. Voices shattered in his head, reducing themselves to a stew of meaningless syllables. The thick yeasty smell of beer had become a stink thick enough to make Dale feel smothered, pinned in place by other people's alcohol. Getting to the door would feel like wading through gelatin.

And he'd sweated through his shirt. Again.

Dale's senses felt choked with fog, his brain stuffed with cotton.

Relax. Nobody's watching you. Nod, smile, and make your way to the door. That's the advantage of not having any good friends here. Nobody's going to worry when you walk out.

Maybe he could find Ritchie tomorrow.

It was a chance.

Dale made it two whole steps before someone shouted his name.

Pure habit stopped him.

Keep going! Pretend you didn't hear.

No, you stopped, it's too late.

He should have kept moving.

You idiot.

Dale looked around.

An unfamiliar kid at a crowded table in the back of the gloomy bar waved. "Dale!" A few words followed, with "prime number" somewhere in the middle of them.

He'd offered drinks for prime numbered cards, yes. But he was exhausted. His every nerve ached. Especially the big mass of them inside his skull.

But a man was dead.

Dale was thirty-two years old. He was an adult. Surely he had the willpower to hold his busted brain together long enough for one more try.

Dale took a deep breath and plunged back in. "Folks, I'm beat. This is the last set, okay?" He didn't even bother to decipher the names thrust at him, just nodded and smiled and said *I'm Dale nice to meet you* until the assault stopped.

To Dale's surprise, the prime-numbered key card belonged to Dora LaCroix. "So it's prime. What's going on?" she demanded, leaning forward to rest her elbows on the round table. Her arms looked as bony as her face.

"The boss said to buy drinks and make friends," Dale said. "He didn't say who to buy them for. So I made up a game."

One side of her mouth quirked up. "Cute. But I don't" *something* "buy me drinks."

Dale raised a hand. "No problem."

"But you look like" *noise noise* "six-hour code review." She pointed at the lone empty chair. "Sit down a minute."

Maybe resting a moment before walking back to the residence hall would be a good idea. The fatigue wasn't just in his brain. Dale's body had taken all the stress it could accept.

He really had to drop that weight. Tonight's dinner hadn't helped.

No—focus!

One last group. Check for numbers.

One check, go to bed.

Seven people. But he'd talked to at least one of them earlier. And some of the other faces looked familiar. Had he already checked their numbers? Or had he just seen them earlier in the day? It didn't help that the con attendees clustered around certain phenotypes.

Stop flailing. Sit down. Check numbers. Go to bed.

He sat.

"Prime" *noise noise noise* someone said, fumbling for his key card. "Dammit, no."

Dale inhaled deeply through his nose.

When he'd heard his name being called, he should have started walking again. If anyone had challenged him tomorrow, he could have honestly said that he was just too tired.

The thought of being caught out—of people finding just how badly messed up his brain really was—repelled him. A whole new level of exposure.

He'd need every trick to get out of here.

Dale thought back to his college days. Before he'd gotten the ADD diagnosis. Before he'd found that atomoxetine kept the symptoms away.

Triage time.

Discard everything he didn't need right now.

Turn off the eyes. Let them unfocus. Keep them open, but ignore the lights and colors.

The humidity-sticky varnish on the chair? Ignore that.

His own headache, his uncomfortable body?

Not relevant. Shut it out.

The only thing that could expose him, the only way he'd betray that he wasn't a normal person like everyone else, was how he responded to what people said.

Focus on the words.

There is no sight. No touch. No smell.

Someone said, "That's not the point. It's the principle of the thing." Better.

He could do this.

"How much have you had to drink?" someone said. Was that directed at him?

Silence.

It must have been aimed at him. Dale opened his mouth. "Either too much, or not nearly enough." Did that sound normal?

"Dude, man, I hear" *something* "bought, like, a dozen drinks. Tell me" *noise* "haven't tried to keep up."

That had to be for him. And what kind of bastard was making him process junk words like *dude* and *man*? "No," Dale said. "Mostly tonic water." All tonic water, really.

That's fine, though. Keep thinking I'm drunk. Drunk is normal.

"Wasn't there another number you were checking for?" a third face said.

Dale had to think a moment. "Yeah. Multiples of 29051. My key number."

"Hey!" another voice said. "I win."

Dale said "I'll get you one with," who had won who had won who had won "Miss LaCroix." No, wait, she hadn't wanted it. And he needed—"What was your number?"

They answered.

Dale concentrated to assemble the sounds into numbers.

Eight. Seven. One. Five. Three.

Dennis Ritchie's number.

Dale's heart leapt and his mouth opened but he needed his eyes now, he'd never recognize that voice again so get those eyes working even though people are clapping all around making noise so thick it's like fog, like mud, scrambling everything even worse but focus *between* those clapping hands. Strip the clamor away.

A card held up in a hand. The hand is on an arm. Follow the arm back up to the shoulders, the head, the face.

I know that face. Dinner, last night. A duck.

Dale's brain screeched like it was full of loose rust.

A Git-hating duck.

Mallard. That was it. Mallard.

Brian Mallard was Dennis Ritchie.

And maybe a killer.

41

Mallard shook his head and waved a hand. He said something about winning and a prize. He must be turning down the drink. Dale shrugged and said "Another time."

A few of the people at the table stood, bantering back and forth. Dale deciphered a few words: dorm, tomorrow, early. One of the men hoisted a glass, but one of the standing guys shook his head.

They must be heading back. I think.

"I think it's time I go to bed," Dale said.

LaCroix said *bzzt brrt* "good idea."

One of the people waved for Dale to follow, and they left as a group. Somehow Dale managed to trail them through Ottawa's Monday night traffic back up to the Byward University residence hall. The churning mass of science camp junior high school kids rampaging in the lobby felt like a whirlwind of noisy flying bricks, but he forced his way through and up the elevator and into the blessed silence of suite 1309.

The suite's easily-cleaned industrial furnishings struck Dale as the most welcome thing he'd seen all day. Even the undertone of industrial-grade bleach cleaner soothed his nose.

Best of all, the door to Deck's bedroom stood open and the light off, revealing an empty bed.

Dale was alone.

He leaned against the suite's door, hugging himself and trying to slow his ratcheting heart. *It's okay. They thought you were drunk, not that you were brain-damaged. Drunk is normal. Drunk is fine. You were a hell of a lot better off than some of those guys.*

The tremble still rolled up his spine and down his arms.

He hadn't had anything that bad since the sixth grade, when the whole school did that week-long winter camping trip and he'd been stuck with his classmates for five whole days. He'd kept sneaking off into the woods around the camp until he could handle things again. The teacher's notes had infuriated Dad, and it's not like Dale could explain.

Dale hadn't thought about that trip in years. For good reason.

He didn't need to be thinking about it now, either.

Unfortunately, Ottawa didn't have a forest to slip into.

Dale did have half a suite.

And Deck seemed the sort to stay out drinking as long as the bars would let him. What was closing time in Canada, anyway? Two AM? Canada was known for beer, maybe they stayed open all night. He could look it up.

Dale unclenched his fists. *Get a shower. Clean pajamas. Check email—no, don't check email, read your book. Slow down. You'll be fine. Soak in the silence.*

Somewhere a door slammed.

The suite door vibrated against his back.

Fine, the almost silence.

A kid's high voice drifted through the door.

You have earplugs. Use them.

The sound of water striking tile and the sensation of tiny hot streams against his skin soothed Dale. Yes, it was more noise, but it was meaningless noise. His brain didn't have to interpret it, so he could let the shower warmth and babble obliterate the world beyond.

He could have spent hours scrubbing the world off his skin, but with Dale's luck the bathroom door would slam open and Deck would spew into the toilet. Once he was clean, he pulled on the pajama pants, staggered into his room, and shut the door.

The desk chair fit under the door handle. Dale added his suitcase and, for some serious weight, his laptop bag. If anyone tried to force that door, he'd hear.

Tomorrow, he damn well *had* to get all his pills. Every one.

Maybe he should take extra.

No, he'd overdosed on atomoxetine once. He didn't need to feel that panic, and he was already sweating sufficiently, thank you very much.

Besides, if he was going to figure out who killed Lash, he needed a clear head.

No, he needed to be able to understand the sounds coming out of people's mouths. Which might be a problem now.

Dale told himself he'd left in time. This should pass by morning. Once he got his morning pills, they'd help. If he had trouble, caffeine would help too. A whole bunch of caffeine. He might not sleep well tomorrow night, but the next morning he was going home. He could be sick on the plane. It'd serve the airline right, for offering such a horrible way to travel.

Slow down. You're okay.

You're better off than Lash, anyway.

And he'd learned that Brian Mallard had a card that could open any door in the residence hall. Like the obnoxious Pokotylo and BSD Godfather Bob Matheson. Any one of them could have been the thieves.

All he had to do was find out which one.

Unless it was someone else.

No, slow down. Test your theory before you throw it away. Don't jump around like the ADD maniac you are.

He tried to read, but the words jumbled on the e-reader screen. Instead, he turned off the lights, closed his eyes, and focused on his breathing.

The last time he looked at the clock, it said 1:08 AM.

Then someone was pounding on his door.

42

"Hey roomie!"

Dale sat up straight, blinking. His brain sloshed in his skull.

Morning light slanted through narrow gaps in the curtain. Crud filled the corners of his eyes.

The voice cut through the door. "Roomie! You up?"

Deck. How late had the man stayed out? And how could someone sound so irrepressibly cheerful after a drunken binge?

Dale tried to answer, but coughed instead. His mouth tasted like a possum had died in there. Last week. He cleared his throat. "Yeah?"

"You up? Con starts in half an hour."

Dale coughed. He'd somehow forgotten to set his alarm. No, not "somehow," he knew perfectly well how he'd forgotten. He was lucky he'd remembered his room number. "Right." His mouth felt painfully dry. "Uh, I'll be a few minutes. You go."

"Right-o." Deck's voice was loud enough to feel like a brick against Dale's tender head. Thankfully, the suite door slammed seconds later.

If Dale was going to have a hangover, couldn't he have at least gotten a drink first?

Wasn't something important happening this morning?

He had to talk to Mallard and try to figure out if the man had a motive for wanting Lash dead.

He should talk to Pokotylo and Matheson again. If they'd killed Lash, maybe they'd say something to trip themselves up. Hercule Poirot and Miss Marple always caught killers in an inconsistency. Some little thing the killer said at the beginning of the book didn't fit with their actions, and at the end the detective would announce to everyone in the library "Aha! It was you!"

Real life didn't work that way.

At least Dale had understood Deck's words this morning. He hadn't permanently fried his brain or anything.

But there was something else…

His talk!

His talk had been rescheduled.

Dale glanced at the clock.

In forty minutes, he had to stand in front of a room full of people to talk about networking via the rooftops of abandoned buildings.

He hadn't had his meds. Coffee. Breakfast.

Plus, the pajama bottoms would make one heck of an impression. Especially with his flabby gut hanging over them.

Dale threw himself into motion. He assaulted his mouth with his toothbrush, yanked his underwear on so quickly he nearly did himself a grievous injury, grabbed the first clean shirt from the suitcase—no, he needed to wear the Detroit Network Services shirt, it was the least he could do if he was going to spill his employer's secrets in public, not that any of this was secret but still.

His sneakers were still a little damp from last night's sweat. Too bad.

Three swipes of a comb through his hair, yank the chair and suitcase away from the door, grab the backpack—was it always that heavy?—

182

check for the room key in his wallet and go—no, wait, passport! He was in another country, he had to carry his passport or the Immigration Police might cart him off to jail. A very polite Canadian jail, but jail.

Discombobulated, Dale got himself out of the residence hall and onto campus. The clear, fresh June air and bright sunshine felt like further insults to his headache, and every step renewed the ache in his joints. Yesterday's kids had disappeared, probably eaten by one of the buildings, so he had a clear shot to MacDonald Hall and the conference.

Yesterday had been rough.

No matter what, he had to take his pills.

Had he brought them? His pulse rocketed before he could remind himself that yes, they were in his backpack.

Maybe they'd fallen out, back in the room.

He should stop and check.

No, no time. The conference had flown him out here and put him up, he pretty much *had* to give his talk on time. He knew he'd put the pill bottle back in the bag right at breakfast yesterday. The heavy backpack bounced against with every half-running step down the nearly empty walkway, giving its own little chorus of jingles and clatters.

One of those rattles had to be his pill bottle.

Dale found MacDonald hall easily enough, tromping hurriedly up the stairs as someone else was reaching for the door.

"Hey," the guy said. "Careful, you're gonna trample someone there."

Dale lurched to a halt. An embarrassed flush joined the heat already on his face.

He'd already sweated through this shirt. He should have packed a spare in his bag.

The guy—Surge, it was Surge. He held a cardboard drink tray in one hand, thumb in the empty spot left by three steaming cups of Tim Horton's finest. "You okay?"

"Yeah." Dale panted. "Talking first."

"You've got a good ten minutes." Surge reached for the door. "And this morning, with the schedule change, nobody'll care if you're five minutes late. Don't give yourself a heart attack." He stepped aside, door in hand. "After you."

"Thanks," Dale said.

The stone-clad front chamber of MacDonald Hall was just as impressive as yesterday. The monitor on the wall still announced the BSD North schedule. But the crowd was perhaps a third smaller than the day before, and the people who were present mostly moved like mummies freshly raised from their crypts. Mummies preserved by vast quantities of beer rather than an embalmer's art. The collective hangovers made everyone's voices quiet and tenuous, as if a shout might break something. Or someone.

The wall clock said Dale had nine minutes.

He heaved out a breath. Nine minutes was enough. He could snarf something from the buffet. A cup of that appalling coffee. Where was that Tim Horton's, anyway? Maybe he'd go for a walk after his talk. A great big cup of decent coffee piled on top of his atomoxetine would snowplow through the crud filling his brain.

First things first: his pills. Understanding two words from his suitemate didn't mean he'd comprehend anything anyone else said. If he got them in his gut now, they might start to take effect before the end of his talk, when people would ask questions.

Dale detoured to an empty wooden chair next to the door and dropped his backpack. He thrust his hand into the side pocket, fingers questing through cables and adapters. No pill bottle. Maybe he had left them in his room? Or just lost them? No, calm down, the bottle always weaseled its way to the bottom—and there it was.

Dale couldn't take his meds on an empty stomach, but he stuffed the morning dose into the knee pocket of his cargo pants for easy access.

He'd forgotten the tablet, damn it. He'd have to use his phone to check the conference schedule—annoying on the tiny screen, but not really a problem.

Not looking at faces, Dale slipped through the crowd to the buffet. The coffee had a queue, as did the hot pans, but the tower of fresh pastries sat unguarded.

Dale glanced at the clock.

Eight minutes.

Today's pastry were cinnamon rolls. Not just any cinnamon rolls, but icing-drenched gooey monsters the size of two clenched fists. If he ate one of those he'd have to get by on, maybe, carrots at lunch. Celery. Some pebbles from the parking lot.

But: no time for the line.

Grimacing, he snatched a paper plate and tonged a gooey cinnamon roll onto it.

Not having time is just an excuse. You know that, right? You just want *a cinnamon roll. Be honest, at least!*

Really, though, he didn't have time.

"Oh, be honest!" someone said loudly behind him.

Dale turned.

"I am being honest," said familiar-looking overweight man a few feet behind Dale. The guy's beard was the most memorable thing about him. That's right, he'd sat next to Dale at the bar. "We need to talk this through. Give everyone their chance."

The guy stood in a ring of half a dozen people. They'd obviously been talking, but right now a few of them were stepping back to give the conversation space. Like they wanted out but couldn't quite manage it.

"Talk it through?" the first voice said.

Dale blinked. He knew this guy. Mister Duck, no, dang it—Mallard. Also known as Dennis Ritchie.

The last of Dale's list of suspects.

Mallard continued, "This whole harassment *policy* group is overblown. Someone needs to tell Hellman that his friends are dickbags, that *he's* a dickbag for defending them, and that if he wants to stay part of SkyBSD he'll bloody well start pretending to be a decent human being. What's so hard about that?"

"Lash was saying—" the bearded man started.

"Lash was saying the same thing!" Mallard snarled. "Don't give me that 'I'm so reasonable' crap. Freedom of speech means you're free to be a jerk. The project is free to throw jerks overboard. We are *not* going to start the whole harassment policy discussion over! Are you kidding me?"

Well, that was Mallard's stance.

But Dale didn't have time to listen. Six minutes until he spoke. He lifted the cinnamon roll and took a bite.

Pure carbohydrate sugary goodness exploded in his mouth.

With cinnamon.

And butter.

He needed a napkin. Badly.

But this was the best cinnamon roll—no, the best *thing*—he'd tasted in years. *Years.*

Dale chewed and swallowed as quickly as he dared, chanting to himself *take your pills take your pills take your pills.* If he let himself get distracted, he'd forget and start his talk without the meds and that wouldn't end well.

If he was sentencing himself to bugs and gravel for the rest of the day, all in the name of getting his meds, couldn't he at least slow down and enjoy his crime?

Four minutes.

And he still had to get his laptop hooked up to the projector. Dale had wanted to review his slides one last time, but that wouldn't happen. He had to tell the story about Will and the seagulls who'd adopted the Van Dyke Tower radio, that'd get a laugh, but he couldn't name Will. Maybe call him Bill. No, too similar to Will, he'd slip up. Fred?

Mallard stormed angrily off into the main lecture hall.

Mallard's departure left silence in MacDonald Hall's vestibule. His outburst had ended every other conversation between the stone-clad walls. The silence even echoed off the domed translucent ceiling three stories overhead.

Dale choked down his pills, without water, and reached for a napkin. *Mission accomplished. Maybe coffee? Nobody could complain about you having coffee during your talk?*

Through the quiet, a distant voice shouted "How could you?"

Dale looked around.

Other people were looking around, just as confused.

The smell of cinnamon and sugar still filled Dale's nose. He was already in trouble with food today. Maybe a second roll? He had the pyramid of cinnamon rolls to himself at that second; nobody'd ever know that the fat guy had taken seconds.

Or thirds.

All he had to do was reach out a hand.

Far overhead, wood snapped.

Metal clattered.

Above him, someone shrieked.

Dale looked up.

He had just enough time to realize the shadow growing beneath the skylight was a human figure, arms and legs waving.

No, not growing.

Plunging.

And screaming.

Half a heartbeat later, haloed in a rain of broken wood and metal balusters, Rob Deck crashed into the heap of cinnamon rolls.

43

The folding table snapped in half around Deck's impact, each half rebounding into the air.

Dale stood, stunned.

A cinnamon roll bounced greasily against his glasses.

More mauled cinnamon rolls rained around him, pattering to the marble tile in sticky smears.

The broken chunks of table landed with a clang.

Then a scream pierced Dale's eardrums.

Dale tried to look around to see who it was but he couldn't. His jaw was locked open, his neck rigid, inflexible.

It was him. Dale was screaming.

Everyone was going to look at him.

He had to get away. Had to stop.

Stop making a scene.

But his feet were riveted to the tile.

Dale dragged his hand up and tried to cover his mouth, but it wasn't a hand, it was his fist, and it wouldn't fit between his teeth and the room was starting to turn gray around the edges like the cinnamon butter on his glasses was thickening but that couldn't be happening except it could right here in the Twilight Zone.

Hands grabbed his shoulders.

Dale tried to recoil from the touch, but more hands were on his other side, firm hands.

They tugged, not roughly. Just hard enough to shift his feet.

"You're gonna pass out," someone said.

"Breathe," said another voice.

Dale's chest felt like someone had welded an iron band around his ribs, crushing his lungs flat. His pulse thudded in his neck and echoed in his head.

"You're okay," someone said. Same someone? Another? No way to tell.

The iron band broke. Dale sucked in great whooping breaths.

"You're okay. He missed you."

"Barely, but" *something something* "you."

"You" *noise* "breathe out too, mister."

something "chair. Just sit" *noise.*

More weight on his shoulders.

Dale let himself be guided into a chair.

So embarrassing.

A man is dead and you're embarrassed? You are such a complete *loser, you know that?*

He had to get control of himself.

Dale squeezed his eyes shut and held his gut like his arms were the only things that might keep him from exploding.

It's time for your talk. You better go get started!

Hopefully whoever was around him would mistake his broken laughter for sobs.

44

Dale took a shaky breath and opened his eyes.

He was sitting sideways on a hard wooden chair right by the MacDonald Hall Entrance, one arm over the chair back. Maybe the same chair he'd rested his backpack on to find his meds. His tremulous muscles ached, battered by the quakes that only exhaustion had stopped. Fortunately, he was so out of shape the shaking couldn't last long.

The guy with the ridiculous beard crouched in front of him, nothing but concern in his eyes. One of the nattily-suited Indian guys stood beside Dale, his hand steadying Dale's backpack.

Chaos owned the hall. People paced back and forth, arms waving, voices raised in shouts of distress and fear. Everything rippled through the butter and frosting smeared on Dale's glasses. His face felt greasy too.

"The police are coming, the police are coming, the police are coming!"

"That's not first aid! That's not" *something* "intensive care!"

"—third floor, it" *noise* "the—"

"—my God, oh my—"

The bearded guy leaned painfully close to Dale's face. "Keep breathing. You're gonna pass out."

Right. Breathe. Dale sucked in a breath.

The bearded guy's coffee breath burned Dale's sinuses.

No, the guy wasn't really that close. Not rudely close. But right then Dale's personal space extended a mile. Maybe two.

"That's better, dude," the Indian man said. "Air is, like, good."

Dale relaxed his chest enough to gasp out, "Sorry."

"Nothing to be sorry about," said the bearded man.

The Indian man gave a strained laugh. "Dude, you were so close, if you'd been loading your plate he would have, like, landed on your freaking hand." He tried to laugh again, but it sounded strangled. "If that'd happened to me, I'd have, like, needed new pants and they'd be calling the janitor to handle a brown and lumpy." He shifted his hand to squeeze Dale's shoulder, right over the backpack strap. "You're rock solid, dude."

For once a touch was comforting, not intrusive.

"Freaking *rock* solid," the Indian said.

Dale felt as solid as one of the gelatin mold skyscrapers Grandma made every Thanksgiving, and almost as transparent. "Thanks." His tongue felt desert parched. "Is he… he…"

The bearded guy nodded. "He's dead."

"They don't know that, dude," the Indian said.

The bearded guy looked up at the Indian. "Living people don't bend that way."

Dale shuddered.

"Sorry," the bearded guy said.

"'s' okay," Dale said. "I, I knew. I mean…"

"Yeah," the Indian guy said. "But sometimes you gotta ask. Just breathe, dude. You'll" *noise* "better."

Dale tried to calm himself. Yes, he was dropping words from what people said—but his meds hadn't had a chance to kick in yet. And almost getting crushed by a three-hundred-pound hacker plunging to his death was stressful enough, nobody'd blame him for acting a little weird.

Everyone in the room would be acting weird.

They're both your suitemates, dude. Every suitemate you've had is freaking dead. DEAD.

You're going to wind up doing life in a Canadian prison. You know that, right?

"What happened?" Dale managed a moment later.

The bearded guy said, "He fell. The third floor mezzanine. The railing broke."

"I don't know how," the Indian said. "I mean, like, shouldn't it be stronger than that?"

Dale had never visited the third floor mezzanine. The dealers were up on the second floor, and he hadn't seen any reason to go higher.

But he found it hard to believe that a public university would be have shoddy railings. The should be able to support even a big guy leaning on them.

Unless, maybe, someone shoved him.

45

The bearded guy introduced himself as Rum. The Indian's name was Pavel. "Like, my folks wanted a real American name, you know?"

With a few minutes of stillness, Dale felt like he'd recovered enough to move if he had reason. Maybe "the building is on fire" or "the zombie rats escaped the lab." Until then, he decided to stay planted on the uncomfortable chair by the entrance, letting the sweat dry on his shirt and the half of a cinnamon roll in his gut churn itself into acid around his meds.

He couldn't help giving a little chuckle.

"What's so funny?" asked Pavel.

"I think I've finally given up cinnamon rolls for good," Dale said.

Pavel snorted, but Rum laughed outright. "That's a diet you'll stick to."

Dale took off his smeared glasses. His shirt had a dry patch, near the bottom, where he either hadn't sweated into it or the sweat had dried. His efforts only swirled the butter and cinnamon around the lenses.

"Here," Pavel said. "Let me."

Dale wanted to say no.

Pavel's face screamed of a need to be helpful, a need to do *something* in the face of Deck's death.

Dale winced and handed the glasses over.

Pavel's fuzzy form produced a foil packet from his laptop satchel. The sharp smell of alcohol split the air. "Here you go, good as new."

The lenses were as clean as the mirrors of an orbital telescope. The wire frames felt pristine over Dale's ears. "Thanks." Apparently natty dressers knew how to clean things.

"No problem, dude." Pavel looked sad. "Glad I could" *noise* "something." *Do*, it had to be *do*.

"You did," Dale said. He glanced at Rum. "Both of you. Thanks."

Rum looked somber. "Little enough."

"Hey," Dale said, thinking furiously. "If you hadn't come over I would have, I would've fainted. Right on top of poor Deck. Face-planted, right there. And there's *no* coming back from that. Really, I owe you one."

Pavel gave a feeble smile. "Like, any time."

The outside door swung open. Two uniformed police officers stormed in.

The system was taking over. Dale leaned against the side of his chair and closed his eyes.

Two murders in two days?

Warren Lash, member of the SkyBSD Senate. He worked on the storage system and the virtual file system. He'd been around a long time.

He'd even done the SkyBSD's original source code management system conversion from the ancient CVS to the more modern Subversion. Lash had been a Subversion guru, from what Dale had heard. And he'd taken point on the harassment policy, an ugly issue that wouldn't make him any friends.

Dale's gut had told him that Lash's death had something to do with the harassment issue.

But Deck's demise blew that theory apart.

Deck was part of CoreBSD, a completely different group of people. They had their own issues, sure, but any SkyBSD policy changes wouldn't affect Deck's people. Each open source group defined their own rules, their own culture.

As far as Dale knew, Lash and Deck had only a few things in common.

They both worked on operating systems.

They both liked a beer now and then.

And they had both been his suitemates.

Slow dread oozed into Dale's already churning guts. Were these deaths somehow… about him?

46

More police officers came into the grand hall, looking far more serious than yesterday's officer. Two claimed places by the door, keeping anyone from leaving. Dale watched Hellman, cigarette pack in hand, argue forcefully but ineffectively with one of the officers.

Let the police deal with it, dude. Lash dying might have been an accident, but two deaths in two days? They can't miss that this isn't normal.

They were your suitemates, but this has nothing to do with you.

Nothing.

Dale wished he could believe that.

It's not like people sitting next to you were done in, is it? A sniper missed and hit your neighbor instead?

Dale would have really liked his own room. Would the cops see that on his face?

Even if someone was going to murder you by dropping something on you from three floors up, that something wouldn't be your roommate. They'd use something more sensible. Like an anvil.

It's not you.

"People!" someone shouted above the murmuring.

Langton stood halfway up the stairs to the second level. His face looked pale, his shoulders slumped, but he had his chin bravely raised as he shouted. "People!" As the noise faded he said, "The officers have asked that we move into the main auditorium so they can work."

"That's us," Pavel said.

Dale's grabbed the back of the chair and heaved. To his surprise, his rubbery legs firmed enough to hold him upright. The crowd shuffled in a wide arc defined by hard-faced police officers, down towards the side hall.

He couldn't help glancing over where Deck had fallen. Between the EMTs he glimpsed a figure shrouded in dark plastic, surrounded by a hailstorm of cinnamon rolls.

The police guided the crowd around to the lecture hall's back entrance. The crowd was definitely smaller than it had been this morning. Dale guessed that the police weren't letting anyone else into the building. Were the BSD North attendees who'd arrived later gathered out on the walkway and sitting on the lawn? Or had they adjourned to the pub or something? Maybe gone back to bed to pull coarse sheets over their faces and sleep off monster hangovers?

Some of the attendees were probably still in bed. They could have set alarms for noon, planning to see the afternoon sessions.

Dale felt a sudden surge of jealousy for those lucky, ignorant people.

He claimed a chair at the end of the center section of the last row, so he wouldn't have to squeeze past anyone else and so he could hopefully get a little bit of space. Rum took a spot a couple seats further down the same row, while Pavel snagged a chair one row down. Their careful glances annoyed Dale. He couldn't blame them for being worried, true, but he was fine.

Deck was the one to worry about. Dale just needed some quiet.

His stomach still burned. Something to drink would help, but he wasn't about to go get a bottle of water from the buffet.

Maybe he'd check his email, once the crowd finished filtering in and everyone was settled. A really ridiculous customer complaint was what he needed right now. Something to take his mind off of Deck, and Lash, and his indigestion, and the police looking at the residence hall registrations.

His stomach burned more fiercely.

Down at the front of the lecture hall, Langton stood next to two police officers, head cocked with listening. The male officer had the body of a weightlifter and had the eyes of a hunting falcon. The smaller female officer had short dark hair and a familiar freckled face.

I talked to her yesterday. I told her about the cyanide. Dale gritted his teeth. *What was her name? Seeton? No, that's the old lady art teacher detective. Sayers? No, no, no. Get your brain off British mystery novels, this is real life!*

Some of the conference attendees had sat next to each other, but most claimed spots with an empty chair or two next to them, naturally diffusing to maximize their personal space. The thought relieved Dale; he didn't look so standoffish back here.

Pavel glanced over his shoulder, saw Dale catching him, and looked away to extract his laptop from its satchel.

You should smile next time. Tell the guy you're all right. That way he'll leave you alone.

Up at the front of the room, Langton was nodding at the cops.

The female officer stepped to face the room. "Take a seat everyone. I'm Officer Senese of the Ontario Provincial Police." Her voice carried to every corner of the room without the microphone.

Senese! The reminder of her name loosed the smallest knot in Dale's neck.

"My partner is Officer Pyre," Senese said. "He'll be moving through the room to collect everyone's name and address. As he does that, think about people who were in the lobby this morning but who aren't here now. We need their names as well."

"Are we being detained?" someone in the front row called. Dale had heard the expression before. It might be right to challenge the police at times, but this wasn't one of those times.

"Not unless you require me to," Senese said.

"So we are free to leave?" The speaker was a ridiculously fat, bald man sitting sideways in the last chair of the bottom row, almost exactly opposite Dale. And yes, he was following the libertarian "get out of jail" script.

Senese rolled her eyes. "You are witnesses to an accidental death."

The question "accident?" grumbled disbelievingly through the room. People glanced at each other.

"People!" Senese shouted. "So far, this is a tragic accident. We are very much aware that your Beastie conference has suffered two deaths in two days. We are investigating this in depth and with all seriousness. Out of respect for your friend Mister Deck, please wait for my partner to collect your information. I understand that a Mister Matheson is organizing something out on the lawn until the lobby is cleared. Once Pyre has your name, you may join them."

The ridiculously fat man in the first row glanced around the room for support.

Dale tried to transmit the phrase *You're an ass* through his glare.

The man looked at the floor. Dale could feel his impotent glower from the other side of the room.

"Thank you for your cooperation," Senese said, staring directly at the man.

Officer Pyre scanned the room as if deciding where to start. He eyed the fat jerk in the front row, then deliberately turned to the far side of the room and started marching up the stairs. Dale felt sure the officer would leave that man for last.

That put Dale near the beginning.

"While Officer Pyre is gathering information," Senese said, "refrain from using cellphones, laptops, or other electronic devices."

Dale groaned, the noise drowned by a hundred other snarls and moans.

Oh, right. Kill someone, lock us in a room, but don't take away our email!

"We'll finish as quickly as possible," Senese said firmly.

Pyre tromped up next to Dale and turned to the opposite side. Dale heard him quietly asking the man's name, address, phone number, and where he was staying. Innocuous enough questions. He copied the information from the man's dark red passport. Which country had dark red passports?

At least the room was quiet. Dale's pulse was dropping. The throbbing in his brain grew softer. Even if Pyre went across the rows, rather than down each section of chairs, Dale had enough time to relax further. Hopefully enough to stop dropping words.

A moment later, Pyre turned from his first man and straight at Dale.

Dale breathed deeply, trying to relax. Get it over with. Good. Simple questions.

The conference might even want him to give his talk out on the lawn. That would be, well, not fun, but memorable.

"Name?" For such a big guy, Pyre had a voice like a hamster. "And ID?"

"Dale Whitehead." Dale felt a surge of relief at remembering to grab his passport on his way out of the dorm.

"Dale Whitehead?" Pyre said.

"Yes, sir."

Pyre's eyebrows furrowed together. "The detective wants to talk to you."

47

Pyre escorted Dale to the lecture hall's side door and handed him off to a clean-cut officer that looked like a recruiting poster. Dale followed blankly, his throat tight and chest tighter. And how much sweat could he put out, anyway? He hadn't even had anything to drink today!

The Police Youth model guided Dale back to the MacDonald Hall lobby. Of course the detective would be with Deck's body—but did he really want to talk to Dale there?

Dale relaxed a little to see that Deck's body had already been removed. Trampled cinnamon rolls covered the floor in a greasy sheen of abused frosting, the sickly-sweet smell gagging-thick. Two janitors lounged nearby, awaiting the command to unleash their buckets and carts.

Thankfully Dale's escort stopped at the doorway and called "Detective Moore?"

A man in a well-worn suit looked up from his conversation with a portly man in shirt sleeves and bright red tie.

"You sent for Dale Whitehead?" the kid said.

Dale tried to still his mind, but fears sprouted like weeds. Had his changes to the registration system made him a suspect? Or maybe the residence hallways had hidden cameras and they'd seen him slip into someone else's room? No, it had to be that he was Deck's suitemate.

The detective exchanged a final word with the other man and strode towards Dale. His polite smile looked practiced, as if his morning routine included running ten miles and then standing before a mirror and painstakingly rearranging the hard planes of his face to bend the edges of his lips up. "Detective Moore," he said, extending a hand.

"Dale Whitehead." The detective's hand was just as hard as his face.

"Thank you for taking the time for me," Moore said.

Dale blinked. He'd had a choice? "Uh, sure."

"The Dean tells me that room 102 is open. Down this hall?"

Dale nodded. *He's asking me easy questions. Getting me used to answering them.* "Yeah, I think so." Wasn't that where the routing talk had been? No, that was 103. "I think it's that one."

Moore fell in beside Dale, with the young officer trailing them. The detective smelled of a spicy cologne. Dale thought it would usually smell okay, maybe even nice, but at the moment it made his stomach knot further.

Yesterday, crammed with computer geeks, room 102 had looked institutional. This morning it looked barren and industrial, built for easy cleaning. Abandoned scrambled eggs and a half-eaten apple sat on the table closest to the door, next to a paper cup of the con's awful coffee.

"This will do nicely," Moore said. "Mister Whitehead, have a seat. Put your backpack" *something*. "Make yourself comfortable. There's nothing to worry about."

That gap—*on the floor*? *By the officer*? No, those were too long. *Down*, it had to be *down*. "Uh, yes, sir." Dale set his bag on the table opposite the abandoned breakfast and plopped into the aisle seat. The morning's barrage of adrenaline had left him sore. His gut hurt from the acid, and the front of his brain had the hollow, distant feeling that foretold a killer headache.

Moore grabbed the instructor's rolling chair and pulled it to the opposite side of the table, so he could face Dale. He leaned back in the chair, spread his hands, and said, "Tell me how you know Rob Deck."

Dale shook his head. "Langton asked me to move into his suite yesterday. He introduced us. Uh, he knocked on my door this morning and woke me up. And he invited me on a pub crawl last night."

Moore nodded. "Did you go?"

"No, I… I was pretty much done in. They were going to hit, what was it? A dozen pubs in Byward Market?"

"This is what he called the 'Pub Crawl of Doom?'"

"That's it."

"Why would he invite you if" *bzzt* "didn't know each other?"

That gap had to be a *you*, that was an easy one. And was Moore implying that Dale was lying? "He invited everyone. It was in the con IRC channel. And he…" Dale frowned. "I think because I was his suitemate. He called me 'roomie.'" Had Deck even bothered to remember Dale's name? No, maybe he was just as overwhelmed as Dale and trying to cover for losing Dale's name. "He—the con puts new people in with people who've been here before. I'm guessing Langton asked him to make me feel welcome."

"Right," Moore said.

Near the door, the young officer's shoes squeaked on the tile floor. Dale's trepidation grew.

"And how did you know Warren Lash?" Moore asked.

Dale shook his head. "I just met him in line, at check-in. He's, he *was*, my suite-mate too. Really, I didn't know either of them before—"

"Relax, Mister Whitehead," Moore said. "I have no reason to believe that you were involved in either death. It's my job to ask questions and figure out what happened. It's clear you were nowhere near either person at the moment they died."

"I was by Deck," Dale said automatically. "I mean, he was alive when he… was…" *falling.*

A shudder ripped up Dale's back.

"Quite," Moore said soberly. "So it's a coincidence. Coincidences are" *something* "common in these situations. But I have to ask."

He makes sense even with the gap, he probably said really *or something like that. Calm down, you'll only make it worse. Detour into detail. Tell him you understand.*

"It's like troubleshooting a network," Dale said. *Relax those shoulders. Unclench your hands.* "You have to gather all the data. And there's always weird things that're unrelated, but sometimes they're the key evidence."

"Exactly," Moore said. "So what do you know about Mister Deck?"

"He's with CoreBSD." What had Deck said. "He did something with VFS."

"VFS?"

"Virtual file system layer." At Moore's blank look Dale said, "It's where everything that's storage-ish comes together. Disk, memory, all of that. It's probably the hardest thing in the kernel."

"Did you do anything with this VFS?"

Dale shook his head.

"How do you know he worked on it, then?"

How *did* he know that? Dale had to think. "Last night. He said he'd needed to drink after doing a lot of VFS work. And he's on the mailing lists, on the VFS discussions.

"All right then. What else?"

Moore's gaze seemed painfully intent. Dale closed his eyes to block it out so he could think. "Seemed like a nice guy. I'm sorry he's dead."

"All right then. What about Mister Lash?"

Dale took a deep breath and opened his eyes. Moore's gaze was just as focused. "He was on the SkyBSD Senate. That's, uh, the people elected to actually run SkyBSD. They don't really run it, though. Mostly they settle arguments."

"So he's a manager?"

"No, he's a programmer. Everyone in SkyBSD's a programmer."

"Are you in SkyBSD? Or CoreBSD?"

"No." Dale saw no need to mention Surge's thoughts that SkyBSD might want him. "I sent some patches in when I hit a problem, but that's it."

"So what did he work on?"

"He was the point man for coming up with a new harassment policy. He did some VFS, I think. Clocks."

Moore's eyebrows went up. "They both did VFS?"

"Yeah, but it's totally different."

"What's the difference?"

"SkyBSD's VFS doesn't look anything like CoreBSD's. They both derive from the original Berkeley stuff, but that's decades back."

"Did Mister Lash and Mister Deck know each other?"

Dale shrugged. "It's my first time here. No idea."

"All right." Moore slowly leaned forward to rest his elbows on the table.

The shift made Dale feel weirdly pressured.

"Did you notice anything else strange?" Moore said.

Someone stole Lash's spare laptop, then I used my illegally hacked room key to escape. Yeah, that'll go over well.

Moore seemed to perk up at Dale's hesitation.

"Just…" Dale's heart felt like a small animal scrabbling to escape his ribs. "They seemed like really nice guys. I mean Lash, he told me where the opening night bar was, and he introduced me to a couple of people. And Deck invited me out on the CoreBSD pub crawl. They… tried to make me feel welcome."

"I'm sure they did," Moore said. "One last question."

Dale tensed. Poirot—no, Columbo, that was the detective that sprung the trick last question. He nodded.

"Yesterday, you told Officer Senese that the chemical supply closet was unlocked." Moore's expression didn't change, but Dale felt the man's increased interest. "Why?"

Why would Moore ask? "It's stupid." Unless—maybe they'd done a tox screen on Lash? How long did that take? On TV shows those came back in an hour, but in a novel they took a week or two.

Moore nodded. "We all are at times. I won't hold that against you."

Dale licked his lips. "Lash turned bright red. Old mystery novels, they say that's… cyanide." He studied Moore's face for even the hint of a smile.

The man's face didn't twitch.

"So I went to look. And the chemical storage closet, up on three, it was unlocked."

"You said this" *something something* "first time here," Moore said.

Dale didn't need the missing words to piece that together. Nodding was safe.

"Chemical storage isn't on the map. So how did you find it?"

Dale's muscles tightened, everywhere, all at once.

He'd promised Hellman he'd leave the guy out of it.

It didn't matter that Dale had discovered that Hellman was the reason the SkyBSD folks had decided they needed a harassment policy. He'd *promised*.

But not only was a man dead. Now a second man was dead.

"The guy who showed me... he'd had some trouble with the school. I was kind of freaked out, and he thought he'd show me the chemicals were all locked up. We got up there and saw it was unlocked, and he, he freaked out too. He asked me to not name him."

Moore nodded. "I can" *something bzzt something* "different now. You need" *something.*

Tension made Dale's brain increasingly, making Moore's words increasingly incomprehensible.

And really, there was only one decent choice.

"Hellman." Dale closed his eyes. "I think it's James—no, Jason? Jake, maybe? But Hellman."

The worst of the tension evaporated, leaving malaise. He'd broken his word—for a good reason, but he still didn't like himself for it.

And he hadn't said anything about the theft of Lash's spare laptop, because his escape implicated him.

"Thank you, Mister Whitehead," Moore said. "When" *bzzt* "you leave Ottawa?"

That was better, but Dale needed a few moments of quiet to get his ability to understand people back. "Tomorrow morning."

"Thank you for your cooperation, and" *noise* "a safe trip." One side of Moore's mouth twitched up. "Do try to enjoy the rest of your stay in Ottawa."

48

In front of MacDonald Hall, the sun glared down from a baleful blue sky. Dale squinted and raised a hand to shield his abruptly aching eyes. The morning's chill and humidity had burned away, replaced with a drier heat that promised to suck the cool clamminess from Dale's skin. His stomach still burned with indigestion and his back ached with the weight of his backpack.

Plus, he hadn't checked his email today. His boss was going to be annoyed.

Maybe he could find a spot to do that now.

Heck, maybe he'd leave the con entirely. Nobody could blame him. What would they say? "He almost got killed by Deck's fall and was interrogated by the police. How dare he not show up to give his talk? Maybe the police kept him?"

That was, if the con even bothered to reschedule his session.

Or any of the sessions.

Maybe he should go to the bar. Not the Royal Oak, which seemed to be the BSD North hangout, but some other bar. A bar with Internet but without much light. He could sit in the corner and check his email and read news until they threw him out. He was supposed to buy drinks. He could buy a lot of them. Go back to the residence hall at 2 AM, stuff everything into his suitcase, and get a taxi to the airport. Airports were pretty empty overnight, and if he showed up before the morning crew, so what?

Forget solving Lash's murder. Or Deck's. The police owned it now.

Just go. Don't even speak to another person.

Dale rubbed his eyes to get sunlight's sting out.

The clearing outside MacDonald Hall was full of nerds.

Maybe three hundred people filled the sprawling grass between four towering stone-clad lecture halls. About half of them faced the broad, sweeping stairs leading up to the biggest building. Bob Matheson stood near the top of the stairs, arms outstretched as he spoke, the godfather spellbinding his adopted family.

A ripple of laughter spread through that crowd.

Other little knots of people stood on the sidewalk, crowded pebbled concrete benches, or sprawled on the lush green grass near flowerbeds.

The roar of a passing tandem bus crept between the buildings. Matheson paused until it faded, then kept going.

The guy had been beyond wasted last night. And today, he tried to entertain half the conference? Amazing.

Then someone almost as skinny as a skeleton appeared right in Dale's face.

Dale jumped back.

Gerry Peterson retreated a step and spoke.

It's okay. Concentrate on the sounds. Build them into words.

"Sorry," Dale said. "I'm a bit shook up."

Peterson spoke. Dale painfully captured each sound. "I can tell. What happened?"

How could he not know what had happened? "Deck died."

something something. Focus! "…mean, with the police?"

"Oh," Dale said. "That. I was Deck's suitemate. And Lash's."

Peterson's eyebrows rose, tightening the skin of his unhealthily gaunt face even more.

"Just a coincidence," Dale said. "That's all. I just… need to chill a minute."

Peterson nodded. "Everything's cancelled" *noise* "lunchtime. Doctor Matheson is telling stories of the old days, or you can just relax."

Before? After? Maybe until, *until lunchtime* made the most sense. "Thanks."

Dale slipped past Peterson and studied the square. Across the square, Matheson was making a heroic last stand to entertain people and keep them from... panicking? Drifting away? Breaking down in sobs? Peterson had already snagged another person coming out of the building; he'd obviously appointed himself Greeter of the Refugees.

The thought of slipping away suddenly felt shameful.

Deck and Lash's deaths were ugly. They'd stressed Dale beyond his tolerance.

No—Dale had stressed himself beyond his tolerance. He hadn't been required to take on the "Find Lash's Killer" Quest. Talking to all those people last night had been his own stupid idea.

No—coming here in the first place. That's where he went wrong.

But now the police knew what Dale knew.

Most of what he knew.

His conscience was clear.

Clear-ish.

Go back to his room? Get a dry T-shirt?

If he saw his bed, he'd never return. The air out here was warm, his shirt would dry. After Deck's death, he wouldn't be the only person who'd sweated a gallon this morning.

Stay here. If he couldn't save Lash and Deck, if he couldn't solve their murders, at least he could bear witness.

Dale studied the square. Exhausted and hung-over geeks occupied all the benches. Conversations clustered on the stairs and across the lawn. The knee-high wall surrounding the raised bed of decorative purple cabbage looked wide enough to perch on and was unoccupied, but it was right in the sun. He wouldn't be able to see the laptop screen. Plus, sunburn.

A couple of teenaged girls in *Byward Tech Youth Camp* shirts scurried down the sidewalk, staring with wide eyes at the BSD North crew. One whispered to the other, who immediately shook her head and started walking faster.

Dale shook his head. He'd officially joined the Scary Old Dudes.

Right up against the side of MacDonald Hall, the sun left a few feet of shade. It would disappear later in the day, but should last until lunchtime. And next to the wall, he might get WiFi.

Dale lumbered down the sidewalk and claimed a space between the beds of bright tulips, where the grass went right up to the building. The stone façade was pleasantly chill against his warm back, and the grass was cool but not damp.

And a thread of signal from the conference internet penetrated the building's walls.

Shrinking his world down to the seventeen inches of his laptop screen bled away more tension than anything else could. Dale dropped the burden of trying to piece together sounds into words, abandoning his ears entirely in favor of his email's clean clear white text on a black background.

Dale skimmed each automated status email, effortlessly correlating information from dozens of disparate systems into a mental image of the company's digital health. A web server had reported a couple of minor errors, but one of the better helpdesk techs had already picked up on it, run a diagnostic, and verified that the company had a spare hard drive of the right sort on hand. Harry was a promising guy—in his early fifties, but eager and quick to learn. Dale needed to spend some more time with him. Maybe offer Harry a couple bigger responsibilities and see how far the guy could go.

But Dale couldn't face talking to Harry right now. The thought of picking up his phone and calling the office, calling *anyone*, made him feel exhausted.

Finally Dale wrote "This looks right. Good job of diagnosis." He went to send the message, but the mail client wasn't coming up—no, wait, he hadn't actually exited the text editor. He needed to hit a colon before issuing the save command, and now he had a couple of lines of garbage in the body of the email.

He hadn't done that in years.

With deliberate concentration he went back, corrected the message, saved the text, and sent it.

Thankfully, the boss hadn't been there. He could hear Will now. *Why do you use vim for emails anyway? It's a Bronze Age text editor.* Every time Will said that, Dale answered *It's not vim, it's nvi.* Or maybe *it's an elegant editor, from a more civilized age.* Which wasn't really an answer. Will wanted to know why Dale didn't use a modern email client, something run with a mouse and with a Send button.

It all came down to: Dale's brain was wired a little differently.

At BSD North, he was completely surrounded by people whose brains were wired a little differently.

Too bad he didn't really fit in here, either.

Dale felt more alone than ever. He couldn't wait to get home, to the familiar discomfort of his regular life. To bring noise to the apartment that now stood silent.

The next page of messages had an email from Will, right at the end. Sent only a few minutes ago. The subject read ARE YOU OKAY?

Dale normally answered email at night, before breakfast, and even while running the electric shaver over his face. He'd promised to not answer email on the toilet. Today, he hadn't been online all morning. No wonder Will was worried.

But the body of the email contained a web link. Dale didn't recognize the site. Some new phishing thing? No, the email headers said it came from Will. Curious, Dale opened the link.

The Ottawa Guardian. "Canada's Capital's Fastest News."
The headline screamed TWO DEAD AT BYWARD U.

49

You've stopped breathing, you idiot. Stop it. No, start it. You know what I mean. You idiot.

Dale deliberately inhaled and exhaled. The sun had crept onward, its rays baking his feet inside his heavy black sneakers. He'd have to move sooner than he thought.

But at that exact moment, most of him still had shade.

And what to tell the boss?

I'm fine. Two people died in front of me.

I was almost crushed by a falling Deck, but came out okay.

All is sunshine and roses.

Instead he replied with *I am OK. Police are here. Everyone is safe.* That should hold him.

The article was typical Internet journalism, light on facts, heavy with supposition, and in desperate need of spell-checking. BSD North was "a gathering of some of the world's leading computer experts." True enough. Warren Lash, age 40, from Utah, "dead of a supposed seizure yesterday morning in MacDonald Hall's main lecture hall." Robert Deck, age 44, from Moose Jaw, Saskatchewan, "plunged to his grisly demise from MacDonald Hall's third floor mezzanine." The article called two deaths so close together suspicious, but the police spokesman told the Guardian that "while we're investigating these tragic events, we have no reason to suspect foul play."

Dale frowned. Detective Moore hadn't acted like a man who didn't suspect foul play.

The article went on to say that Byward University was well-known for hosting scientific leaders from around the world, and that regardless of the results of the police investigation the university faculty needed evaluation. The Guardian clearly had something against Byward University.

The phrase "yet another example of the incompetent management of one of Ottawa's academic jewels" made Dale's jaw clench so hard that the roots of his teeth ached.

Dale couldn't imagine how Deck and Lash's deaths had anything to do with the university faculty. How dare some Internet rag use this tragedy as fodder for their ongoing feuds?

It'd serve them right if something happened to their site.

Not that Dale would do anything, of course.

What kind of server did they run on, anyway?

No, no.

But it'd serve them right.

How well did they keep their security systems updated? The way these yellow Internet sites ran, someone with the right skills could probably shut them down with one command.

Dale shook his head. No!

Yes, he broke into servers. To hide. That was different. Dale wasn't destructive. If anything, he made the systems he entered illicitly more secure. Yes, that was out of pure self-interest. He didn't want some kid discovering the same flaw Dale had leveraged and exploiting it to trash the system.

He closed the browser to see a reply from Will in his email. *Call me.*

Dale groaned. He'd only started to relax, and the infuriating article had blown that away. His brain couldn't handle any more words right now. Worse, phone calls stripped away some of the sound Dale needed.

Combined, he wouldn't understand anything Will said. Dale chewed his lip a moment, then replied *Terrible signal here. Barely have wifi. I really am ok.*

Will's response appeared in seconds. *If it's bad, come home. I'm sure the conference is a wreck right now. I know you don't deal well with this sort of trouble.*

Dale couldn't help a laugh. Will didn't know just how badly he reacted to pressure. *Nobody* knew.

Yesterday, he would have snatched at that offer. Heck, if he had read that mail before walking out MacDonald Hall's front door, he would have sat down in the lobby and tried to move his flight reservation forward. Right now, though, looking at the sober discussions between the BSD North attendees, the idea of going home early made him even more uncomfortable.

He'd been Lash's suitemate.

Deck had died right on top of him—almost literally.

They were decent people. He owed it to them to at least stick around.

Besides, a nasty little voice in his head muttered, you've got a private room now.

Dale squashed that voice. He could always barricade his bedroom door when he was there. And anyone who broke into his room when he wasn't there deserved all the vile laundry they found.

And if he stayed, he might learn something else. Something to help identify the killer.

Thanks, boss. But I'm fine.

Send.

With the aid of time, a peaceful patch of grass, a building to lean against, and a connection back to the steady, sane world of his machines, Dale eventually slowed his disordered thoughts. The June breeze over his face soothed him more than he'd expected. Weirdly, the other geeks passing by and talking had their own soothing effect. He didn't have to talk with them or pay attention to their conversations to catch that the deaths had distressed everyone in the community. Dale knew he wasn't unique, but it comforted him to see it.

He felt almost normal when someone calling his name shattered his attention. He jerked his head up.

The crowd was funneling back into the building.

Surge stood on the sidewalk, an expectant look on his face.

Dale blinked. "Sorry."

Surge nodded. "Programmer's coma, I know." He looked pale. Perhaps even ill. "You coming?"

At least Dale didn't have to hyper-focus to understand Surge. His brain had started to recover. "Uh, sure. What's going on?"

"Lunch." Surge stood patiently as Dale stuffed his laptop back into the bag. "There's a session in the lecture hall in half an hour."

Dale's laptop needed a charge. The lecture hall would be good.

But how could the conference continue? How could anybody possibly think about software with two people dead? Sure, the lunch was already arranged so they might as well eat it, but the only topic Dale could imagine attending would be a panel called "What the Hell, People?"

To his embarrassment, the thought of food made his stomach grumble.

How could he be hungry? How could he even think of going near the buffet again? It would be hard to get a sandwich while staring up the whole time, looking for a falling body.

You decided to bear witness. You can at least go inside.

Dale suddenly realized his laptop lay half inside the backpack, but his hands had stalled and he was sitting still. He shook himself and stuffed the laptop in, hurriedly zipping the top. He tried to roll himself up, but his butt and calves had gone to sleep. *Look, everyone, the fat guy can't even stand!* No, that wasn't going to happen. He clutched the wall for balance, and a moment later had his feet.

"Grass is a crappy seat," Surge said.

Dale felt grateful for his words, and then foolish at feeling that way. "Yeah."

"I wanted to talk to you anyway," Surge said.

What now? "Sure."

"I've reviewed your bug report history. You've sent us some really good patches."

"Thanks," Dale said. What did Surge want? "It's just stuff I found."

"And you've done it over a few years, off and on."

"I found problems off and on."

"Still, it's a good track record." Surge studied the flowing crowd while Dale stamped blood back into his legs. "I want to officially propose you for a commit bit."

Pins and needles broke out in Dale's legs, but they felt mild next to the eruption in his brain.

More exposure?

He hadn't even thought about his original reasons for coming to BSD North. The deaths had completely swept them from his mind.

If he had direct commit access to the SkyBSD sources, he could make whatever improvements he wanted. Yes, they had to pass review, they had to have purpose, but Dale knew he could do that.

He also knew that he could hide almost anything in those improvements. A minor change to one part of the system, combined with similarly minor changes elsewhere, could give him access to millions of machines.

"I've never sponsored anyone before," Surge said. "But… that's pretty selfish of me. I mean, you seem to have what it takes, and if we don't get new members, SkyBSD will just die—" Surge flushed. "Uh, I mean…"

"I get it," Dale said.

Most of the crowd had funneled into MacDonald Hall's grandiose entrance. Surge looked ready to join the end of the queue, but still watched Dale expectantly.

Source code control recorded who made each change. Eventually, someone would figure out what, exactly, the combination of Dale's changes to SkyBSD and ShufflSoft did. He didn't want his name on them.

But what could he tell Surge?

"I'll…" Dale said. "Let me think about it. This isn't a good day for decisions."

Surge grew even more pale. "Yeah. I know what you mean. I don't mean to push, I mean, I'm not trying to—yeah."

"Yeah," Dale said.

With that, they silently joined the end of the line to see what remained of the conference.

51

The crowd had started flowing into the building, but the motion suddenly stopped while Dale was still on the sidewalk in front of MacDonald Hall. He peered ahead, one hand shading his eyes from the sun.

Surge frowned and pulled his phone from his pocket. A couple clicks and he said, "IRC says this *is* the lunch line. They've moved the buffet out into the middle of the room, and they're asking people to take their meal straight into the lecture hall."

Dale heaved a breath. Nobody would want to stand beneath the mezzanines, or anywhere near them. They could all look up for falling bodies and quickly dash through the threat zone.

Threat zone? What was he thinking? Bodies were *not* going to rain from the rafters.

Dale wished he could believe that.

Once they all had lunch, a bomb in the lecture hall would lower the planet's average intelligence by a couple percent.

Dale tried to relax as the line shuffled forward. Surge seemed to be concentrating on his phone, thumbing expertly at the tiny screen. That saved Dale the effort of trying to make conversation.

Peace.

The next person in line glanced over his shoulder. "Hey."

The man's short hair and the face that looked axe-carved looked familiar. Dale knew he'd talked to this guy during the conference, but couldn't remember where. "Hi."

"How are you doing?"

"Pretty okay. You?" Dale's fresh tension started easing away. He could fake niceties with the best of them.

The guy shrugged. "Better than some."

Dale's laugh sounded like a snort. "Yeah."

"I wonder what they're going to do?" the man said.

"No idea."

"My talk on the CoreBSD mail server was going to be this morning."

The gears in Dale's brain clicked into place. CoreBSD mail server—the man had written the book on it. He'd hidden in front of Dale in yesterday's breakfast line. What was his name? Dale tried to remember his copy of that book, on his shelf in his office. He lived in Malaysia, hadn't he said?

Relief surged through Dale. "Mine too, Max."

Max's eyebrows tilted in, just a little bit. "What were you talking on?" Had Dale upset him somehow?

"Rooftop wireless in abandoned buildings," Dale said.

Max's face relaxed. "That's right. Sorry, it's been a rough couple of days."

"Sure," Dale said.

The conversation stalled. Dale cast around for something to talk about.

Other than the obvious, of course.

"I know that," the next person in line said. "But we have to talk about it some time."

"Sure do," the man standing next to him said in a thick Southern drawl. "But it won't be at this con."

"Then when?"

"What's next? Exeter in August, isn't it? Merry Old England?"

Dale wondered what were they arguing about.

The first man gave an angry snort. "I can't get away in August. We've got a big deployment due before September. And this whole thing is wasting developer time."

"I reckon sticking with Subversion wastes even more time."

Ah. That.

"Changing all our processes to use Git, now that would be a waste of time. How many years have we spent writing and tuning all the custom tools around Subversion?"

Well, Dale thought, listening to them argue is better than some of what we could be talking about.

"Git gets rid of a bunch of those."

"People keep saying that, but I don't see an actual workflow. Version control is what defines our whole community. It's how we work. You can't just burn it down without a replacement."

"Didn't y'all see Donny's talk yesterday?"

"Yeah, I did. It was full of 'to be defined.'"

"The heart and soul of it's there, but—"

"And it changes everything we do."

To Dale, Max said, "I'm glad we stuck with CVS."

"That's one way to avoid that whole argument," Dale said.

The pro-Git man in front of them turned. "What happens when you have to do major repo-wide changes?"

Max shrugged. "We let Deck…" His voice shrank, and his gaze turned down.

"See," the man said, "there's lots of Git—"

"Sir!" the Southern-sounding man he'd been talking with interrupted. "His friend died today. My friend the Subversion expert died yesterday. I realize y'all're spoilin' for a fight, but this is *not* the time. As you Northerners would say, don't be an asshole."

The pro-Git man's face flushed. "Uh… You're right." He looked at his friend. "I apologize. Was just trying to, to talk of something else. Something that would take our minds off of things."

"We're all on edge," the Southern man said. "Don't make everyone else feel worse just so you feel better. And *I'm* not the one who needs the apology."

Mister Git looked at Max. "I'm sorry." He turned to Dale. "Sorry."

Max nodded. "It's okay."

Yelling at us to make himself feel better? That's pretty jackass, but… "Sure," Dale said.

Yeah, the guy had been rude. He'd wanted to make things better, and nearly made them worse.

Dale frowned.

He'd wanted to make things better for himself by getting into the registration, and what he'd learned had nearly melted his brain last night.

He'd wanted to make things better for himself, to prove how smart he was, by getting his changes into ShufflSoft and SkyBSD. He'd wound up witnessing two murders.

The crowd shuffled forward.

Yes, his patches would give him silent access to about one percent of the Internet. Which was cool.

But how was that going to come back to bite him?

Did everything Dale do only make things worse for himself?

"I don't believe we've been introduced," the Southern man said. "My friends call me Willoughby. My loud-mouthed friend here is Dean, but you might know him as Kanga."

Dale didn't know him by either name. "Dale."

"Max."

Dale said, "Any idea what's going to be going on?"

"Not a clue," Dean said.

"We saw the con committee talking about an hour ago," Willoughby said. "They had a cop with them."

"The cops'll want us to stay around," Dale said.

"You think so?" Max said.

"They always say 'don't leave town,'" Dale said.

"That's in old movies," Willoughby said. "I do believe the world has moved on since then."

"And some of us have expensive flights to catch tomorrow," Max said.

Dale shrugged. "I'm not leaving early. That would look really bad."

Max grimaced. Dean nodded. Willoughby pursed his lips but didn't object.

The line shuffled on.

Willoughby looked back at Max. "Since you're here, could I trouble you for a scrap of your mail server wisdom?"

Max straightened. "Of course."

A discussion of SPF records and proper email relay configuration thankfully kept the conversation going until the line crept through the doors and even along the double lines of the buffet tables. With a plate in his hand and a cutlery set rolled in a napkin in his pocket, he kept catching himself watching the mezzanines as his hands filled his plate. The dealers had abandoned the second level, leaving their tables and displays in place.

Nobody stood on the third level, either.

Dale's eyes kept fixing on the line of yellow caution tape up on the third floor, though, where Deck had crashed through the railing. It took all his willpower to walk slowly from the end of the buffet line, beneath the looming mezzanine, and into the crowded lecture hall. He plowed through the overwhelming babble of hundreds of conversations to the first empty seat he saw, about halfway up but inconveniently right up against the glossily-painted cinderblock wall.

He'd barely logged into his laptop when Langton came to the podium. "Find a seat, people. We need to start."

52

The bags under Langton's eyes were deep and heavy enough to pack for a trip to Australia. His voice had none of yesterday's charm or excitement. His hands gripped the podium like they needed to both anchor him and hold him upright.

If something Dale had organized had gone this badly, Dale would be hiding under the stairs with a teddy bear. Langton had to have will of steel.

Or at least aluminum.

People's conversations sank from rolling thunder to a confusing babble.

Dale took the moment to log into the BSD North IRC channel, then to study his plate. His spirits plunged even further.

He'd let his hands fill the plate while his attention had been on the mezzanine. Clearly his hands were trying to murder him, only with calories. Four half sandwiches, medium-rare roast beef and cheddar on thick onion rolls. *Two* little plastic tubs of potato salad? And how had he stuffed half a dozen of those little bite-sized brownies into the middle of all this, like chocolate filling in a giant donut?

He could have made worse choices, but he'd have needed to plan them out in advance.

His stomach growled so loudly at the sight that the chubby nerd sitting next to Dale looked over curiously. Dale gave an embarrassed shrug.

The first bite of roast beef felt like an explosion of flavor in his mouth. And it was real Cheddar cheese, not that awful "pasteurized process cheese food crap" they injection-molded out of plastic.

"Come on," Langton said. "We all want this done with."

Dale frowned. Responses appeared in the chat channel.

jackon> What do we want done with?

BigSpatula> I think we're all ready to go home

FlamingSkul> were all ready for serius drinking

FlamingSkul> SERIUS

Dale felt a little better at that. He wasn't the only exhausted one.

The noise finally fell away. Langton said, "Okay, people. The committee has met. We've made calls to the various sponsors. Overwhelming consensus is that the conference needs to be suspended."

A groan rose from the crowd—not exactly a complaint, but five hundred people giving commiserating grunts or releasing held breath or just saying "hmmm…." A dozen responses flashed by in the IRC channel, mostly supporting Langton's announcement except for that jerk ham11. A few people stirred in their seats.

Dale let go of tension he didn't know he held. At least he wouldn't have to give his talk. A millisecond later, shame at his selfishness flooded him.

But still, he'd learned his lesson.

He wouldn't be submitting any more talks to a big con like this. Dale wasn't the right sort of person for it.

Or for all the deaths.

"Settle down, folks," Langton said. "We still have some business." He waited a breath, then said, "First off, that leaves the question of how to handle the remaining presentations. The speakers all uploaded their slides before we accepted their talk. Speakers, please make sure that your very latest slides are on the con web site. People always make last minute updates. Thank you."

Dale twitched to upload the file immediately, so he wouldn't forget to do it, but he restrained himself. If he opened his web browser, he'd almost inevitably get distracted by something. He'd miss the rest of Langton's talk.

And he really wanted to hear this talk.

"We still want to give people the opportunity to talk with our speakers, and give our speakers a chance to present the information from our talks. But most of us have only one thing on our minds today, and that is our lost friends." Langton struggled for a deep breath. "We all live in different parts of the world. Realistically, we cannot all attend Warren and Rob's services. So this afternoon and tonight will be a wake."

Applause broke out, more restrained than yesterday's tsunami of enthusiasm.

Dale joined in, his relief nearly complete. He didn't really know either Deck or Lash. He could show up, stay half an hour to show solidarity with the truly bereaved, and go find a quiet place to wait out the clock until his flight.

He didn't need to subject himself to the grueling flood of people he'd tried to handle last night.

"We'll be giving our speakers a red name badge," Langton said. "Speakers, we're asking you to hang around the wake for a few hours and give people a chance to talk with you about your topic."

Dale's neck and shoulders tightened like someone had cranked the invisible knob controlling their tension a quarter turn. His spirits fell again.

It's not so bad. You can sit in the corner. Will this place have corners?

"Sadly, the Royal Oak can't hold all of us," Langton said. "We've called the Irish Arms. They have no scheduled events this evening, so they'll be calling in extra wait staff just for us. The wake starts at four PM."

Dale glanced at his computer for the time. The IRC channel already said:

twist3r> three hours

The Irish Arms had a whole bunch of dark corners. Maybe he could get there early. Claim one of the tiny two-person tables. He'd be there, but throttle the number of people he had to interact with simultaneously.

Don't be such a wimp. You can do that.

"Next order of business," Langton said. "Irregardless of what happens with BSD North, we need to maintain positive relationships with our sponsors for other BSD events. Remember, this is all live-streaming, and being recorded for posterity. I'm going to take a moment to thank them before we proceed."

Langton lumbered through a few slides on the big screen, speaking with all the energy of a first-time marathoner who'd just staggered across the finish line. Dale wondered just how much a "platinum sponsor" had to pay to have their name mentioned, and what they'd think of this performance, but didn't want to distract himself by checking.

ham11> lame laaaame

MrToast> have to do it. you don't want other con's funding to dry up do you?

ham11> still laaaame

Dale wanted to type *have a little respect*, but he had no idea who ham11 was or how he'd take such a comment. A poorly chosen word here would probably turn the whole channel into a flame war.

Langton finished his trudge. "We really do want to thank all our sponsors for their support of BSD North. This con would not have been around for fifteen years without them." He raised his hands to clap twice.

Perfunctory applause rose, then quickly died.

"People have asked what's going to happen next year," Langton said. "The answer is, I don't know." His shoulders somehow drooped even further. "I've run BSD North since the first year. I need to think about next year. Please don't push. When I make a decision, I'll let you know."

Dale couldn't help the surge of sympathy. Langton had clearly put a lot of energy into building a successful conference.

If Langton hadn't started BSD North, maybe Lash and Deck would have died anyway.

But they wouldn't have died here, in front of everyone.

Dale could see that toxic knowledge freighting on Langton's heart.

"Next up, Marina Strch—" Langton coughed. "MDS has asked for a moment, on behalf of the SkyBSD Senate. And no, this isn't their usual thing. Please give her your attention."

BigSpatula> what's this?

ham11> you kept saying wait and we'll find out. wait and we'll find out.

Dale had seen MDS with Lash when they'd been checking into the residence hall. Her clothes seemed even more rumpled, but she seemed to be making an effort to stand straight, with square shoulders, as she marched to the podium.

"Thank you," she said.

Dale watched MDS.

MDS watched the room.

An unbearable moment later, she leaned into the microphone. "Yesterday, Warren sent us one last email." Her thick Eastern European accent gave her voice gravitas, as if she was addressing the assembled United Nations. "Thanks to our graylisting, it didn't arrive until later in the day. Warren recommended that we form a committee of SkyBSD committers, composed of volunteers approved by the Senate, to act on inter-developer harassment claims. He recommended that we hire outside experts to counsel us in these cases."

More clapping came, this time interspersed with a few loud catcalls.

MDS let the tumult die at its own speed. "This contentious topic has been argued at length. The Senate is not expecting the arguments to end. As long as people have been able to talk, we've argued about proper behavior. In the circumstances, the Senate feels compelled to give Warren's plan a try. We have officially requested the SkyBSD Foundation provide funding to hire expertise as needed to advise us in these cases, and they have agreed to do so."

More polite applause came, laced with catcalls. Dale suspected the people complaining were the most likely to wind up in front of such a committee.

Dale felt glad that Lash had gotten his last word out on his last project.

And couldn't help wondering what the killer thought about it.

He glanced around. While some people looked annoyed by the announcement, nobody seemed especially infuriated.

What do you expect? Someone to shout "you mean I killed him for nothing?" Sheesh.

MDS studied the room. "That is all. Spasebaw."

Langton took the microphone back. "Right. That just leaves us with the highlight of BSD North, the auction."

53

Auction?

How could they have an auction after the deaths?

Dale reached for a little plastic tub of potato salad. Three of the half sandwiches had evaporated while he'd been listening to Langton. He didn't have the energy to be annoyed about it, though. He'd almost been crushed by a falling body this morning. The warm soothing carbohydrate glow already starting to radiate from his center was the only comfort he had.

Eating was a terrible way to cope with stress. Just terrible.

Salads for a month after this. You'll wish for bugs and gravel. As a treat.

He found it hard to care about the future, though.

The hard plastic seat dug into his thighs and the edges of his back. He abstractly knew that overeating would just make that worse—but that was a problem for tomorrow.

He had to survive today first.

"We had originally planned to vote on a charity for the auction," Langton said. "After discussion, the committee and I propose that we use the auction to benefit the newly formed BSD North Warren Lash and Rob Deck Memorial Fund. All proceeds will be divided evenly between their families."

This time the applause split the air. Dale joined in, clapping hard enough that his palms burned.

Langton let the applause roll on for a moment, then raised a hand to quiet it. "That's pretty overwhelming, but I should ask if anyone objects."

"I have a question," someone called.

In the second row, four or five rows below Dale, Surge had his hand up.

"Yes?" Langton said.

"Is this fund only open for the auction? Or can we donate?"

"A slide with donation information will go up at the end," Langton said. "We'll take anything auction losers want to donate, but we're hoping with an auction we can raise enough to help their families cover…" His mouth twitched. "Expenses."

The spontaneous applause was even louder this time. Dale ignored the sting in his palms to join in.

Langton glanced around the room. "Committee members, did I forget anything? No? Okay, then, here's our first item." He rustled in a bag and held up…

A pen? Were they going to auction off junk?

"Mister Hessler donated this fine pen," Langton said. "He first bought it at the BSD North auction two years ago, for—what was it? Sixty dollars?" He peered into the audience. "Yes, sixty dollars. He donated it again last year, and won it for one hundred twenty. He's kindly returned it for a third go, and frankly, I think it needs a new owner."

Okay, that was kind of funny.

"Do I hear twenty dollars?"

"Thirty!" someone shouted.

Challenges flew from around the room.

"Fifty!"

"One hundred!"

"Two hundred!"

Langton's pointing finger bounced around the room, trying to home in on the bids as they came in. "I have two hundred," he said. "Two hundred going once… going twice…"

"Two-twenty-five!"

"Three hundred!"

"Three hundred! Going once. Twice." Langton studied the room. "Sold, to Mister Hessler. Congratulations."

Dale's caged tension finally ruptured into a laugh as he joined the rest of the room in applause. The same guy had purchased that same pen three years in a row, for more money each time. Dale couldn't help wondering what he'd pay for it next year.

If there was a next year.

Langton said, "Next up, a rare and exotic item. Something that was in high demand." He held a gray T-shirt up in both hands. "It's a BSD North T-shirt… from last year. Do I hear twenty dollars?"

"Twenty!"

"What size?" someone shouted.

"Thirty?"

Another person called, "What size?"

"It's size…" Langton fumbled at the tag. "Size triple-X."

Dale surprised himself by shouting "Fifty!"

Dale didn't worry too much about money. And the shirt was his size. It was a good cause. Why not?

"Sixty!"

"Eighty!" Dale shouted.

"Ninety!"

"One hundred!"

How high would this go? He had a sudden vision of himself shouting *one billion dollars!* with his pinky pointed at his mouth like a James Bond villain parody. "One-twenty!"

The room grew quiet.

"I have one twenty," Langton said. "Going once. Twice. Sold, for one hundred twenty!"

Applause erupted.

Dale flushed again. *You just spent over a hundred bucks on a T-shirt? You gonna start going to those expensive shops and buying their limited edition Ts now?*

Shut up. Dale started to rise to claim his prize. *Just… shut up, you jerk, it's for charity.*

"Come down at the end of the auction," Langton said. "Gerry, are you getting all this?"

In the front row, gaunt Gerry Peterson raised a pencil and said, "Who was that?"

Langton said, "Dale Whitehead. One of the speakers."

How did Langton remember Dale's name, with all these people?

Langton added, "Dale was scheduled to talk on wireless networking on top of abandoned buildings in Detroit. He installs routers without any local power supply or infrastructure."

Dale suddenly became very aware of all the faces turning to him. A few people leaned to whisper to each other. His face grew uncomfortably warm.

"Dale, are you coming to the Irish Arms later?" Langton said. "I'm sure people will want to hear you talk about that."

Why not just put a freaking spotlight on me? "Uh," Dale said. "Yeah. I'll be there."

A couple of the people weren't just looking at him, but studying his face.

Like they planned to track him down later.

Dale wanted sink into invisibility.

But Langton started the auction back up, pulling the crowd's excruciating attention away from Dale.

The auction wasn't all T-shirts and pens. Hardcase Systems had brought a small demo server for their exhibition table, and had donated it to the auction rather than return it to the United States. The server's list price was twenty-five hundred. The auction shot past that, stalling at ninety-eight hundred dollars. Just before Langton announced the sale someone in the back offered an even ten thousand dollars. The applause that greeted a five-figure price sounded like a herd of elephants, and Langton needed a full minute to restore order.

"Now," Langton said, digging in a bag, "here we have a rare and exotic, one of a kind, business card for my last job…"

Dale laughed with everyone.

He wasn't going to bid on anything else. Not a chance he'd invite that kind of attention again. But once they put up the donation information, he could send some money in. With a hundred twenty for the shirt, he could add another one-thirty and make it an even two hundred fifty dollars for the fund. That would make a dent.

"Sold! One-fifty for my business card, to Dora LaCroix!"

Dale clapped. If a business card was going for one fifty, maybe he should up his donation. He could afford three hundred.

"Next up, a special edition of Donner's book on NFS version four. I'm told only five copies of this edition exist? Yes, five, and only in print—no ebook. I'm not going to say the new title, because this is being streamed live and recorded, but he's put all the swearing back in."

Dale couldn't help laughing with everyone else.

Despite himself, he was having fun.

Not enough fun to make up for the stress.

Or for Deck and Lash.

But fun.

"How much have we raised so far?" Langton said.

"Thirty-one thousand, nine hundred, and nine dollars," Peterson shouted.

The loudest applause yet broke out.

"That will help their families," Langton said. "And I'm out of auction items. If you have anything else, we'll put it on the block."

"The right next year to sponsor decent coffee!" someone shouted.

"An extra hour at the bar tonight!"

Someone else called something, but Dale's mind was already exploding.

54

The last two days whirled in Dale's brain.

Time.

Lash's body arching from its chair, in the front of this same lecture hall.

A half-eaten Danish tumbling from his thrashing grip and onto the table.

It was all about time.

A mysterious voice behind the closed door of Lash's bedroom.

Deck saying, *I have to talk to that bastard.*

Columns of data from the registration system.

Rules exist to be exploited.

Mallard saying *Hey! I win!*

It could be.

Timing.

It could be that simple.

Dale's hands scrabbled into place on the keyboard. He shut Langton out, his neighbors, every sound, in favor of a web search.

He'd been right.

Time.

His shaking fingers switched to a terminal window, where he went to the files containing his downloaded copies of the residence hall data.

He had had suspects: the folks who had key cards that could open any door.

But he had another list of suspects… if you allowed time.

Dale had watched them talk.

Heck, he'd downright coveted their common bond.

And the two lists partially overlapped.

Never mind that his he'd listened to everyone on his first list. A murderer had to be able to cover up his feelings. And someone who could kill a friend might even get twisted pleasure out of getting all that sympathy for the death of his friend.

Dale ran a couple commands to grab information from the downloaded dump and tried to dump them right into another command. His mouth tasted like acid, and his heart was beating so hard that his pulse seemed to knock his fingers astray on the keyboard.

Slow down. You've been typing for thirty years. Take an extra two seconds and don't screw this up.

Dale made himself breathe, used the up arrow to bring his last command up at the terminal prompt, and skipped through it to make the corrections.

His stomach burned, but his blood ran cold.

Check the other names. Don't rush this.

The results? Weird… but they fit.

All he needed was one bit of corroboration.

And three people in this room could provide it.

And for this, people were like time servers. If you had one data source, you had to blindly trust it. With two data sources that differed, you couldn't tell which to trust. But three? If one of three differed, you threw it away.

Unless there'd been a conspiracy.

But Dale couldn't believe Lash and Deck had died by conspiracy. If the BSD community was given to murderous conspiracy, they'd have died out decades ago.

Everything fit.

Dale's chest felt tight, as if his ribs were contracting around his lungs. Adrenaline cast bright sparks at the edge of his vision. He suddenly realized his right toes were drumming maniacally against the tile floor.

He needed a discrete effort of will to stop the foot.

And to breathe.

Dale looked up.

Langton was speaking again, holding a single battered shoe at arm's length. "I have four hundred! Come on, folks, a little higher and we can get the total up to 32678. His families deserve that."

Dale felt surrounded by aquarium glass. The auction, the BSD North attendees, even his terrible plastic chair felt like they were in a different universe, just a little bit off from his own. He wasn't here. He wasn't really involved.

But he was involved.

How was he going to do this?

Could he do this?

The data fit.

But if he was wrong…

If he was wrong, these folks wouldn't welcome him back. That was all right—he had no intention of ever leaving Detroit again.

But the event was going out on the Internet. Live.

It was being recorded. It'd be on the Net forever.

If he was wrong, the few minutes of video where he made ridiculous claims about respected people would shroud him for the rest of his career.

Will wouldn't fire him from Detroit Network Services. Will was too nice, and cared too much about people. Dale had planned on remaining there forever.

But no company lasted forever. What would happen if DNS went away in ten, twenty, even thirty years? Someone might buy them out.

The big telcos that were planning to deploy gigabit IP over the old VHF frequencies might put all the little folks out of business. Even six months from now, he might find himself queued at a job fair, resume clutched in one sweaty hand.

You can't just sit here and let a killer walk!

He could wait, though. Skip the wake, or show up late. Find that nice Officer Senese, or—yeah, he had the detective's card in his wallet. A phone call. Spill what he knew and what he'd figured out. Let the professionals handle it.

Meanwhile, the killer might skip the wake entirely. Go to the airport.

Leave Canada before he could be interrogated.

Dale had been uncomfortable on the other side of a table from Detective Moore.

He'd have been much more comfortable with a phone between them.

Denial would be a lot easier from California. Or Paris, or Malaysia, or… or wherever these people lived.

But Dale wouldn't have to humiliate himself by standing up in front of all these people. The thought of his talk had filled him with dread. Speaking to four times that many people?

Impossible.

He could learn everything he needed at the pub. Face the suspect there.

If he was gutsy enough to show.

You worry all the time. Your worry makes you do stupid things. You make trouble for yourself.

For once in your misbegotten life, dude, face something head on.

"Four hundred dollars for Mister Dexter's left shoe!" Langton called. "Congrats to our winner, Mister Mosiejczuk. Ask him how to spell that, I'm not even going to try."

Dale's mouth felt parched as sun-baked asphalt.

Give it to the police.

Langton said, "And as nobody else has anything to offer—"

Go straight to Detective Moore once we're out.

Do the right thing for a change, you moron.

Dale spasmed to his feet. "I have something else to auction," he called.

Langton stopped and looked at him.

Oh my God, what are you doing? Sit back down you moron they're all going to laugh at you—career is over, over, you are so dead, so completely dead, this is insane you are not a cop stop it.

The gaze of all the people turning to him felt like a physical pressure. Dale had an irresistible urge to back up against the cinderblock wall, but his feet absolutely refused to move.

Even the silence felt heavy.

Dale tried to lick his lips, but his tongue was sandpaper.

"I'd like to auction off the identity of Lash and Deck's killer."

55

The room erupted in mayhem.

Two hundred separate conversations broke out simultaneously, all at the top of people's lungs. A few people stood up, shouting towards Dale. He winced against the barrage of noise and attention, trying to wheeze a little air into his paralyzed lungs.

Don't faint now. You're committed.

When they prove you're wrong, don't say I didn't warn you.

"QUIET!"

The overhead speakers squealed into feedback. Dale clamped his hands over his ears. The screech faded just as quickly as it had appeared.

At the front of the room, Langton spoke quietly into his microphone. The overhead speaker volume wobbled a bit up and down as he adjusted the volume. "Mister Whitehead. That's an incredibly serious accusation. We joke and have fun in the auction, but I must tell you: that is not at all funny. At *all*."

The lining of Dale's mouth felt ready to crack as he spoke. "I'm utterly serious." To his surprise, his voice didn't wobble at all. He reached for the can of cola.

Quieter babbling broke out around the room. People's attention bounced between Dale and Langton.

Langton held the mic away from his face and took a couple steps forward, to the first row of seats, where Bob Matheson was sitting. After a hurried consultation, no more than ten seconds, Langton stood. "All right, Mister Whitehead." His voice had no flexibility. "I won't be accused of silencing you. You have sixty seconds to state your claim. After that… we have a police officer outside. She'll be escorting you back to your room to gather your belongings and leave campus property. We won't need you to present your work tonight—nor, I suspect, at any other BSD conference."

Dale's innards felt tied in knots. Not just professional humiliation.

Banishment.

And once the video hit the Internet, he wouldn't be welcome in a coffee shop.

He made himself crack open the cola and take a swallow. "I accept."

Langton's hard face didn't move. "The clock is going."

Time, Dale told himself.

In more ways than one.

"One question first," Dale said. "Doctor Matheson."

Matheson looked up at Dale quizzically.

Yes, you. Doctor Matheson. Godfather of BSD. Guardian of the code and *the culture and ethics. You weren't drinking beer last night, but wine.*

This little open source operating system is your life, and you're about ready to retire. When someone proposed making a change, when your chosen successor proposed a change, did it drive you nuts?

You had a key card that could open any building. You, and Mallard, and Pokotylo.

Aloud, Dale said, "Your coffee yesterday. Your Tim Horton's. I imagine you had it made to order, right? With just the right amount of cream and sugar? Just the way you like it?"

The whole room was staring at Dale like he'd gone insane. Down in the front row, Surge alternated between glancing up at Dale and madly typing. Langton gripped the podium like he wanted to stuff Dale inside it and ship the whole thing to the Marianas Trench. Peterson had his pencil in hand, but seemed transfixed by the slow-motion car wreck Dale was making of his life.

In the corner of Dale's eye, the IRC messages scrolled by faster than anyone could read.

"What does that have to do with anything?" Matheson said.

"We all saw Lash—Warren—drop the Danish," Dale said. "But cyanide isn't instant. It takes a minute or two to work. And both you and he had coffee. He had plenty of time to drink it, pick up the Danish, and take a bite. And coffee is *personal*. It's not like a Danish. Who gets which coffee is *important*. So…" Dale tried to make his voice stronger. "Who made yesterday morning's Tim Horton run?"

Matheson just looked at him, perplexed.

No, not perplexed. Stunned.

Dale's shaky confidence dissolved into dust.

The man really had no idea what Dale was talking about.

From the far side of the room, someone said, "Surge."

Dale glanced over.

He didn't recognize the man who'd spoke.

Matheson said, "Surge lost a bet a few years ago. He always gets our Tim's."

Dale looked down to the front of the room.

Surge's face had gone even more pale. He glanced from Matheson to Dale, up into the crowd and back down to Langton.

His gaze met Dale's one last time, eyes wide in… panic?

Between Dale's encounter with the killer and his chance to check the database, Dale had moved to a new room.

Anyone could would have had a chance to sloppily delete incriminating data then. And maybe add a few bogus entries.

Anyone, including Surge.

Surge's hand stabbed his keyboard.

The lights went out.

56

Darkness swallowed Dale.

After the bright fluorescent overheads, the room looked pitch-black. Dale's screen cast a trapezoid of light into the darkness, but the sudden shift left Dale blinking and unable to see anything beyond that rectangle.

The omnipresent, unnoticeable hum of the air handlers died.

In their place, unintelligible shouts rose from the darkness.

Dale would have to squeeze past six other people—and at his size, squeeze was an understatement.

Someone shouted angrily.

A dull thud rocked the darkness, followed by a cry of pain.

People were moving. Panicking. Someone had just gotten hurt—bumping into someone? Falling down the stairs? Or both?

Chase Surge?

Other people were closer. And Surge had muscle. Dale was stubborn, but by the time Dale could get in the aisle, down the stairs, and over to where Surge had sat, he'd be long gone.

Running is stupid. You're dumb, not stupid.

Okay, work with what he knew. How had Surge killed the power?

The network.

Surge must have penetrated the campus power systems. Utility systems were legendarily insecure. Tampering with utilities carried heavy sentences that usually ended in "to life." Merely inquisitive hackers tended to leave them alone in favor of easier targets.

All that frantic typing Surge had been doing?

Queueing up commands. Scripting the power shutdown, and who knew what else.

He'd only had to hit "enter" to fry everything.

Dale plopped himself back into his seat and switched to a terminal.

Messages flew past the IRC window.

twist3r> building cell node is down.

ham11> 911 system just said little italy shooting and officer down they're sending everyone to the other side of town

BigSpatula> building alarm system also down

Dale's eyes had begun to adjust. Five hundred laptop screens cast a murky, spooky multicolored gleam across faces, broken by people trying to get down the aisle. How would he find the power system, get the lights back on?

"I've got him!" someone shouted.

A woman shrieked "Let go of me you jerk!"

Someone cried out in pain, their voice gaining pitch before fading away.

jakon> physical lockdown triggered

ham11> sending 911 signal, will take a minute, doing it legit

Dale quickly switched to another terminal window and brought up his notes on his initial exploration of the Byward University network. Residence halls, computer lab—stay away from that, it'd be the most heavily filtered part of the network—science labs, public safety—

There! He'd captured a couple of weird devices in the list.

You don't know anything about power systems. What do you think you can do?

It can't be that hard. The blasted thing was even running a telnet server, like they *wanted* to get broken into.

And Dale would be happy to oblige.

The banner identified it as a Honeywell such-and-such. Dale ran a quick search on the name—yes, a power distribution controller, with a manual in PDF. The manual's first page indicated it was meant for multi-kilowatt installations. This whole building wouldn't pull a kilowatt.

Just how much power had Surge shut off? This building, or half the campus?

Dale tried to swallow the knot in his throat and ran a quick search of the manual. The Honeywell, like so many other industrial control systems, shipped with a default username and password.

Would he be that lucky?

Dale flipped back to the telnet session. He carefully typed *admin* and *password1234*.

The prompt sat for a moment, then returned *Username*.

Dale clenched his teeth. Why would someone running telnet even *bother* to change the password? If he'd had time, time and warning, he would have set up a packet sniffer and captured the login credentials weeks ago.

Instead, he typed *admin* and *1234password*.

Nope.

Someone shouted, in pain or anger.

Dale thought he heard Langton's voice above the hubbub, but couldn't make out the words.

Something thudded against the front of the room.

If Dale didn't get the lights back on quick, people were going to get hurt.

A shout carried surprised pain.

Hurt even worse, you mean.

And this was all his fault—

No. No time for that. Dale tried half a dozen common passwords in quick succession, trying to get in the power controller.

Nothing.

Think, dang it. You have a brain, you have a great big stupid brain, use it!

flamingSkul> 911 call in. They're on their way.

ham11> how'd you do that so quick?

flamingSkul> you did it legit. ;-)

flamingSkul> dongs. dooooongs

nmbclust> dear WHOEVER IS IN THE HONEYWELL POWER CONTROLLER: single-session device! either get the power on or get out of my way!

Dale involuntarily jerked his hands from the keyboard. He reflexively started to turn to the IRC session, but instead disconnected from the power controller.

Even in the dark, he could feel embarrassment burning his face. He switched to the IRC window.

dsw> nmbclust: sorry, out

nmbclust> ty

Seconds later, the lights hummed to life.

The crowd made one last growl of noise, then fell silent.

Throughout the rows of seats, people stood and sat and sprawled. A really big guy with a beard that could be used to scrub pots crouched on the aisle at the end of Dale's row, holding his strangely bent arm and sobbing.

Down at the front of the room, Surge stood at the door. He had the handle in both hands and feet planted against the floor. He gave one last might yank on the door.

It didn't budge.

Surge slumped.

He slowly stood straight.

Chin bowed, he turned to face the crowd.

Dale's breath stopped.

The whole room fell silent.

"You don't know!" Surge shouted. "I had to! He said we needed too much manpower to handle patches, and that it would just get worse as the community grew! He'd drafted a message, he was going to check it during the opening ceremony and send it out! After all we did to make Subversion awesome, he was changing his vote to support switching to Git!"

57

The whole crowd of the lecture hall froze in shock.

Dale realized his fists were clenched. To his surprise, lava-hot anger was rising from his guts. His breath came quick and hot.

No. Calm. A lynch mob isn't the way.

You started this. You better finish it.

Dale deliberately rose back to his feet. "And what about Deck!" he shouted.

"I didn't mean that!" Surge shouted, sudden defiance in his pose. "He figured it out and grabbed me, so I pushed him. I didn't know the railing was that weak!"

The anger was hot—but somehow almost freezing. Dale felt as if making any movement at all would cause him to burst into flame. Keeping control required stillness.

"You murdered a man over version control systems?" Dale shouted. So much for control.

"It's not just version control," Surge shouted back. "It's how we work. It's our culture. And Git is just—*stupidity*."

Surge whirled and yanked on the door.

"Active shooter control system," someone shouted. "That door's sealed tighter than Oracle's wallet until the police open it."

Surge's expression crumpled. He sagged against the door and put his hands over his face.

Dale's whole body quivered. Surge had killed someone—*two* someones—over software? No, once over software, once to protect his secret. He ached to tromp down the stairs and punch Surge's face until he felt better.

Looking at Surge's obvious object misery, though, gave him the strength to sit back down.

A torrent of obscenities had flooded IRC. Not much different from usual, Dale thought, except in quantity. Other messages appeared at the end.

jakon> I could undo the shooter lockdown. open the door?

The session sat quiet for a long breath.

Finally Dale typed

dsw> Nah. Let the cops handle it.

58

The Ontario Provincial Police patrolman dropped Dale at the residence hall right about dinnertime. Dale felt like he'd been run through an old-fashioned clothes wringer, squeezed absolutely dry of anything useful. He ached to waddle up to his room, drop everything on the desk, take a long shower, and vegetate. Maybe finish that new Rob Cornell karaoke lounge mystery.

But he'd made promises.

Dale compromised. He dropped the weighty laptop backpack, grabbed a new blue T-shirt, threw it back in favor of a black one, and began the trudge down to Byward Market. Surprisingly, the walk went more quickly than he'd expected—maybe because it was downhill, or maybe the evening breeze along the canal was just cool enough to take the heat off him. If it was as cold tonight as last night, he'd stop at one of the innumerable souvenir shops and buy himself a hoodie.

It's not like he'd be back in Ottawa again.

He should get himself something to remember this trip by. It'd be one heck of a conversation starter. *Oh, this old thing? I bought it the time I caught a murderer.*

Not that he could ever tell anyone the whole story.

The road flattened out amidst the kebab shops and vintage clothing stores. Dale made a few left-right turns to get into Byward Market proper and his destination.

The Irish Arms.

The bright sunlight and bustling crowd felt ominous. At any moment, one of the people going by might stop ignoring him and say something. He'd have to form an answer. And after Moore's polite but excruciatingly thorough interrogation, Dale felt unable to compose a coherent sentence.

The Irish Arm's blocky shape looked like it might be a haven. The dim lighting and dark décor made it a perfect place to hide. Even the canvas tent over the broad sidewalk promised shelter from the scurrying crowd.

Unfortunately, Dale knew what waited inside.

You promised Langton. Go in. Tell him you're fine. You're a free man. He's the con chair, he'll spread the word.

Dale gritted his teeth and marched in.

He'd barely crossed the threshold into the tent when a dozen voices shouted his name. Dale leapt three inches into the air and landed looking every which-way.

Langton had staked a claim to one of the rough-hewn picnic tables under the tent, right inside the door. Matheson was with him, bushy mustache miraculously free of beer foam.

Hellman, Duck—no, *Mallard*—and Peterson rose from another table and started clapping.

At a table at the opposite end of the tent, Hellman's mortal enemy Dora LaCroix stood and began pounding her hands together.

Pokotylo bounced up from the back and erupted in a drunken "Woo!"

Then everyone was standing and clapping.

Dale froze, petrified. He stood there paralyzed in applause like he'd been fixed in a block of Lucite.

Seconds or days later, Langton took his arm and shouted, "Okay, folks, that's enough. I think Dale here is about done in."

The applause broke apart, finally fading enough that Dale could breathe.

"You all right?" Langton said.

Dale made himself nod. "Detective Moore was… thorough. Very thorough."

Langton steered Dale to a seat at his table. "Listen," Langton said, running a hand across his smooth pate. "I have to say two things."

"Sure," Dale said.

"First… what I said at the end there." Langton looked embarrassed. "I take it all back. You are absolutely welcome at any BSD conference. Really. And we want you to come back and give your talk some time."

I'm never coming back. I'm never leaving Detroit again. I might never leave my apartment *again. Doesn't Amazon Prime deliver bugs and gravel?* "Thanks."

"Second," Langton said, "I hope you know your money's no good. People are lining up to buy you drinks."

Dale felt his face grow slack. Taking drinks from folks meant talking to them. If he had to talk to a whole line of people, they'd have to cart him off to the hospital in one of those special jackets with sleeves that buckled in the back.

Matheson laughed, but without malice. "Ian, I think our Dale has had" *noise* "about all he can take."

Breathe. You're not going to die if you just breathe. "Uh, yeah."

Langton nodded. "The police can be rough. How about a beer?"

Dale suddenly realized his mouth was parched. The paper cup of water at the OPP station felt like a decade ago. "Sure."

He'd barely said the word when a tall glass appeared at his elbow. Dale sipped it gratefully. Keats Pale. Just like he'd ordered the first night.

"So," Matheson said, leaning closer. "How did you figure it out?"

I thought it was you. "Everything just… added up."

Matheson nodded as if Dale had answered the question.

A woman on the other side of the table held a hand out and said,

"We verified some mail headers," her thin voice freighted with a heavy Eastern European accent. Dale had to blink to focus on her face.

MDS. Lash's friend from the residence hall check-in. She'd looked rumpled at the check-in and downright disheveled at the auction earlier today. The neat T-shirt and hair pulled back into a ponytail made her almost unrecognizable now.

"The mail *was* delayed by the graylist," MDS said. "But the original message, it went out yesterday afternoon. After Warren's death."

Dale nodded. "Surge stole Lash—*Warren's* spare laptop. He stole the laptop from our suite yesterday afternoon. Cut out the part about Git and sent the email."

"It read kind of odd," MDS said. "We thought it was from his late night."

Langton leaned towards Dale. "Listen. I spent all last night, and all today, wondering what had happened. I was ready to shut BSD North down, thinking that we'd never know what had happened but that it was probably my fault. BSD North is happening next year. And we want you to come back. Whether you present or not. All expenses paid."

"Uh," Dale said. "Thanks."

"And just so you know," Langton said, "we uploaded the raw video to YouTube."

"Raw video?" Dale said.

"From the auction. And, you know, after."

Dale wondered if he could sink into the concrete. "Oh."

"A hundred thousand views in just the few hours," Langton said. "Warren and Rob? Their kids are going to be splitting a quarter million dollars for college."

Dale leaned back. Maybe he couldn't have saved Lash or Deck.

But if his face on YouTube took care of their kids?

He'd find a way live with it.

Matheson said, "And this company that offers public Git repos? They sent ten thousand dollars."

Dale couldn't help a quick laugh at that. He buried it in the glass of Keats. The glass was already close to empty.

"Surge talked to us about giving you SkyBSD commit access," MDS said. "He wanted to mentor you."

Another Keats had somehow appeared at his elbow. Dale drained his first glass, the cool richness soothing his aching gut. "It's fine. Really."

"Hey!" someone said behind Dale.

Dale jumped again.

Max Reinholt's hatchet-carved face appeared over Dale's shoulder. His sport jacket was unbuttoned, and a great big beer grin shone on his face. "I know these SkyBSD buggers got you first. They got the seat by the door just for that. But listen..." He rushed a hand up to his face to cover a tiny belch. "The CoreBSD folks are in the back, right behind the bar. We're drinking to Rob—and Warren, sure, but Deck, he was ours. Promise me you'll stop by us."

Great. "Sure." *Boy, that didn't sound half feeble.*

He was never going to get out of here.

"We'll send him back," MDS said. "But right now, he is ours."

Max said, "Just tell me they're not letting you buy your own drinks."

"He's covered," Matheson said. "He's covered for the rest of his life."

Dale shriveled inside. "I'm okay."

Max clapped his shoulder. "You better be. We owe you one—and no, not a beer, not moving house. More the 'you need an international corporate network busted open?' sort of thing. Okay?" Without waiting for an answer, Max weaved his way back.

Dale took refuge in his beer.

"As I said," MDS said, "your commit bit. Surge can't mentor. We want to hook you up with another mentor."

"That's okay," Dale said. The beer really was tasty, and filled a gap in his gut he hadn't noticed before. "I don't need a commit bit."

"Really," Matheson said. "I want to take you on myself."

Dale almost choked.

Matheson laughed. "Yes, I gave up mentoring a couple years ago. But even if you don't fit in the network group, we'll find you the right spot."

"Seriously," Dale said, "I don't need…"

And he looked around the table.

And past his table, where other people sat at other tables.

Everywhere he looked, people were looking back at him… but not because he was an outsider.

This was a family. And they wanted him.

You've never felt included. You've never felt like you belong. Maybe you don't belong. But you know what? These people are asking you to come in. No, they're damn near begging you. What do you want, an invitation engraved on a circuit board?

"When I get home," Matheson said, "I want to spend some time with your patches."

The patches. Dale's fiendishly clever masterwork.

A million new places to hide.

Or, maybe…

One place to stand in plain sight?

"You know," Dale said, picking up his drink, "I think I need to do some work on those patches." He usually felt uncomfortable talking, but somehow, these words came easily. "I was sitting in the police station, waiting, and realized I can take some stuff out of them. Make them simpler. Can I send them tomorrow?"

Matheson smiled. "Tomorrow is fine."

The perpetual knot in Dale's guts eased.

Maybe tomorrow would be fine.

Never miss another new release!
Sign up for Michael Warren Lucas' mailing list at
http://mwl.io.

By the Same Author:
Immortal Clay
Kipuka Blues
Butterfly Stomp Waltz
Hydrogen Sleets
git commit murder

Nonfiction (as Michael W Lucas):
Ed Mastery – SSH Mastery – Relayd and Httpd Mastery –
PAM Mastery – FreeBSD Mastery: Advanced ZFS
FreeBSD Mastery: Specialty Filesystems – FreeBSD Mastery: ZFS
Tarsnap Mastery – Networking for Systems Administrators
FreeBSD Mastery: Storage Essentials – Sudo Mastery
DNSSEC Mastery – Absolute OpenBSD – Network Flow Analysis
Absolute FreeBSD – Cisco Routers for the Desperate – PGP & GPG

See your favorite bookstore for more!

Printed in Poland
by Amazon Fulfillment
Poland Sp. z o.o., Wrocław

50735909R00155